CONNECTING WITH KIDS IN CONFLICT

A Life Space Legacy

William C. Morse

Published by
Reclaiming Children and Youth
&
Starr Commonwealth

CONNECTING WITH KIDS IN CONFLICT
A Life Space Legacy

Author: William C. Morse
Epilogue: Larry K. Brendtro
Editors: Larry K. Brendtro and Adrienne Brant James

© 2008 by Reclaiming Children and Youth & Starr Commonwealth

Printed in the United States of America
By Sisson Printing, Sioux Falls, SD
This book uses acid-free paper.

ISBN: 978-1-60702-673-0

BIOGRAPHICAL INFORMATION

William C. Morse, PhD, (1915-2008) was Professor Emeritus of Psychology and Educational Psychology at the University of Michigan where he chaired the Combined Program in Education and Psychology. He directed the University of Michigan Fresh Air Camp for troubled boys from 1945-1960. After retiring from Michigan, he taught at California State University at Northridge and the University of South Florida. His 60 years of service left an unmatched legacy of former students and professional colleagues who are leaders in work with troubled children and youth.

Larry K. Brendtro, PhD, was a doctoral student of William Morse at the University of Michigan and served on the clinical faculty of the Fresh Air Camp. He is a licensed psychologist and has been a child and youth care worker, teacher, and principal. He taught in children's behavior disorders at the University of Illinois, The Ohio State University, and Augustana College (SD). For 14 years he was president of Starr Commonwealth in Michigan and Ohio. He is founder of Reclaiming Youth International and senior editor of the journal *Reclaiming Children and Youth.*

Adrienne Brant James, MSW, is an enrolled member of the Bay of Quinte Mohawk Nation and founder of Turtle Island Learning Circle. She earned her graduate degree from Wayne State University and was an instructor in the School of Social Work. A close colleague of David Wineman, she served for six years on the clinical faculty of the University of Michigan Fresh Air Camp. She has been founder and administrator of non-profit corporations providing group homes, day treatment, rehabilitation, and alternative schools for persons with special needs.

CONTENTS

Foreword v

Chapter One: *Lasting Impressions* 1

Chapter Two: *Fresh Air Camp* 7

Chapter Three: *Troubled Students* 14

Chapter Four: *Deviance or Variance?* 25

Chapter Five: *Connecting in Crisis* 32

Chapter Six: *Working with Groups* 38

Chapter Seven: *Assessment in the Life Space* 46

Chapter Eight: *Hope Regenerates* 54

Epilogue: *Roots and Wings: Pioneers and Their Legacy* 57

Bibliography 75

Editorial Notations 82

FOREWORD

Chance encounters play a prominent role
in shaping the course of human lives.

– Albert Bandura

Bill Morse often quoted Albert Bandura (1982, p. 747) to explain how unexpected events can radically alter our life story. His own path took a radical turn when he met Fritz Redl, who worked with troubled boys at the University of Michigan Fresh Air Camp. It was also a chance encounter that led this writer to that same camp a generation later. As a young professional, I stumbled on a potent paperback called *Children Who Hate,* written by Fritz Redl and David Wineman (1951). I followed this book to its source and recruited Morse and Wineman as my mentors. Fritz Redl was philosopher king, and we never tired of tapping his expertise.

Four decades later, another chance encounter brought me back into close contact with Bill Morse. I was researching great pioneers in reclaiming youth and decided to gather oral history from my former doctoral advisor. Bill had passed 90 years of age and thus qualified for "pioneer" status. Remarkably, he was hard at work on the sixth edition of *Conflict in the Classroom,* co-authored with another of his former students, Nicholas Long.

A colleague from Fresh Air Camp days, Adrienne Brant James, and I were organizing a major conference at Wayne State University to celebrate the Michigan Reclaiming Model pioneered by Redl, Wineman, and Morse. We decided to publish a small book highlighting contributions of Morse and his colleagues. Bill provided us with an excellent oral history recorded by Rosemary Nagel a few years ago for the Council for Exceptional Children (Morse, 1992). We also conducted our own interviews. Bill was inspired and insightful as we tracked the timeline of his rich career, his life-mate Sunny Morse occasionally adding additional details. Thus this book was prepared for publication in time for the 2008 Roots and Wings conference which would honor him.

Bill Morse died at his home in Michigan on January 23, 2008. He never liked ceremony, so his last book will not start with an obituary. The reader will find Bill's own words sufficient to fathom the magnitude of this man and his contributions. Those who want to know more about his career can read the memorial web site posted by the Council for Children with Behavioral Disorders (Lloyd & Kauffman, 2008).

This project could not have been completed without the determination of Adrienne Brant James, who shared in interviewing Bill and who excavated from the dusty archives of great libraries every bit of information that can be found about pioneers in the Michigan Reclaiming Model. Adrienne also sparked the idea for the Roots and Wings Seminars to be held at Wayne State University in Detroit where Redl and Wineman taught and where she was a student.

This book is published by the journal *Reclaiming Children and Youth* in collaboration with Martin Mitchell and colleagues at Starr Commonwealth in Michigan and Ohio. The following chapters are produced in the same conversational style in which they were recorded by Bill Morse. The Epilogue reviews the related research and practice applications of the Reclaiming model. Our goal has been to capture the ethos of the Reclaiming pioneers and pass their legacy to future generations.

Larry K. Brendtro, Editor
Reclaiming Children and Youth

THE FRESH AIR CAMP KID

This symbol of the Fresh Air Camp appeared on its printed material for over forty years. The original was drawn by University of Michigan alumnus, Angus Babcock, class of 1926 (McNeil, 1962, p. 113).

CHAPTER ONE

Lasting Impressions[1]

*As I look back over the years, I think our greatest success came as
we tried to develop a culture of caring without neglecting the reality of
life challenges: one foot in caring, the other foot in reality.*

I grew up in Erie, Pennsylvania, on the Great Lakes during the
Depression. My father was principal of a junior high school and was paid
in script. We lost our house, but we were never hungry. It was a terrible
time for everyone. You would see people selling apples to survive. Stress
was all over the place. The fear that we would go without was traumatic
for me.

Our family was religious and went to church and Sunday school. I had
one brother three years younger than I. Our parents were quite free with
us and would talk with us about problems. I don't remember very many
times that there was any kind of harsh punishment. We had a lot of
pressure to do well in school, because everybody knew our dad, and so we
were supposed to produce. My mother had been a teacher and was now
managing the household. She was easier to be close to than my father.

My school was small enough that people knew each other. There
wasn't anything like special ed, and all the kids were in the same class. It
was "inclusion" like we're talking about now. I remember all the boys had
to fight a particular kid, who was real big, in order to be a member of the
boys' society. If you didn't do it, you were an outcast and had no friends.
That was hard for me as I had been taught not to do such things.

Most teachers were distant and aloof and only interested in academic
matters. But there was a shop teacher who would hang around after
school and you could talk to him about anything that was on your mind,

even questions you couldn't ask your parents. I don't know if you'd call him a real mentor, but he was quite important to us. There weren't very many teachers like that. You didn't really discuss your beliefs about things, even in social studies classes. You tried to memorize the presidents or whatever they wanted. It was pretty severely content-oriented. Out of maybe 100 teachers, there might be five or maybe ten who were known by the kids as good teachers.

There was a lot of formal discipline but no guidance. Punishment was the main method of discipline, usually by publicly embarrassing students. If you shamed easily, they could manage you very well. Most of us were afraid our parents would be called in if we did anything. But there were a few kids that the rest of us would look at with a great deal of envy because they didn't seem to care what happened. Shaming had no effect.

The first line of discipline was the assistant principal. If that didn't work, you went to see the principal, and that was the end of the line. They would exclude you from school, which a lot of kids, of course, didn't mind. But for kids like me, that was very embarrassing. They would berate you in public and call your parents in. They would talk about how bad you were, what was going to happen to you. It was very threatening. You thought the end of the world was coming if you got kicked out of school. It was a highly moralistic WASP climate.[2]

Cheating was watched very carefully. They had no trust in us – probably with good reason – but the academic climate was repressive. The quasi-vocational courses were different, and those were usually fun and sort of free. They had football and a lot of music and drama. There were good things about school, but it wasn't the kind of place I'd want to replicate today.

Even as a boy, the peer culture impressed me as a significant factor. Teachers think the individual kid comes to their class but there is another whole other set of operations going on. If you were different, peers gave you a hard time. And nobody including teachers ever talked to us about that – except in my family. We were taught to treat everybody the same, regardless of race or ethnic background. That was part of the morality of our family. But that didn't cut much ice when you were in school or out with the other kids.

I grew up with a boy who was obviously different. I think he probably was LD [Learning Disabled] and ADD [Attention Deficit Disorder]. He was physically ungainly and his motor control wasn't very good. He was a very nice, pleasant kid. But I remember being puzzled by the way the group would work him over at times. Whatever peers did to him, it didn't seem to matter. He'd come back. I tried to understand. He was different than most kids, but I used to go to his house.

Two other kids impressed me because they seemed to be different from the rest of us. One of them must have been at the genius level. He was an electronics nut, and that was the first time I ever saw any television. It was about one inch square and was on for one hour a day. If you came over to his house, he'd let you look at KDKA. But I didn't admire the guy's great brains, because intelligence seemed to get in the way of social relations. The other kids gave him a hard time, too.

I remember Mary, who was physically awkward, and we labeled her "retarded." She had a speech problem; her voice and timbre were quite different and masculine. But at adolescence, we couldn't afford to be different, so we'd be very careful and dissociate from her. Mary made her way in life and seems to be as normal as I am or as the next person. But at that time she was different and excluded from the peer culture. Kids like Mary could have very good futures if they could get out of school without being too maimed.

Quiet or withdrawn kids who sat in the corner were ignored. Some were good students who didn't relate to others. They retreated into books and were highly praised even though they weren't happy by any means. The other kids didn't like them because they were DARs: damned average raisers. They didn't interfere with anybody else but we felt they were odd and they were rejected by peers.

I also recall a few emotionally disturbed kids who sometimes would explode in class. They would storm out or swear at the teacher, which was a criminal offense. In those days you just didn't do such things. These threatening kids also would throw rocks at us and each other. I couldn't understand them at all, but they were obviously quite aggressive and impulsive. We learned to avoid those kids, or they'd "gitchya" as the saying goes. Kids all understood this. We had our own private peer culture that had little to do with the culture that the adults thought existed.

After finishing high school, I enrolled in the University of Michigan with two buddies, also sons of principals in our hometown of Erie, Pennsylvania. We aspired to be lawyers and the others stayed with that goal. But I found pre-law courses utterly boring and retrospective. I didn't want to invest my life thinking about solving future problems based only upon the past. I decided to become an English teacher.

When I was a junior in college, I married Sunny. We had first met when we were both in junior high school. She sang in the church choir. I couldn't sing, but I went to the choir. So Sunny and I met in church. That's one thing I give organized religion a high mark for. She seemed to be more thoughtful than most. She spontaneously does helpful things for people. It was her general demeanor, she was a "sunny" person, warm and friendly.

I worked for an English professor and got very interested in literature and drama where the dynamics of the human being are displayed. Sometimes you can learn a lot more from good drama than from psychology textbooks. Drama, which is based upon stories of human conflict, teaches realistic lessons about life.

Shakespeare was a great psychologist – or whoever wrote those plays if he didn't.[3] All of the human dilemmas are portrayed in his works, and the motivations of people are revealed. In *Hamlet*, we see the dark side of human nature. *Julius Caesar* teaches the whole business of power. *Midsummer Night's Dream* deals with fantasy. A more recent playwright who made a big impact was Arthur Miller.[4] All of his dramas are really chunks of life that are exposed, as in *Death of a Salesman*.

I got my teaching certificate but it was the Depression and there weren't any jobs. So we stayed at the university and I started a master's degree in English. But after taking a few courses, I got more interested in psychology. What I wanted to find out from graduate study was: What is the essential element of human nature? Why are some people so altruistic and concerned while others are not? Why do different cultures seem to have such different values? I was surprised to discover that the professors who taught psychology didn't seem to live any more effective lives than the rest of us. By this time, I also had become very skeptical of formal religion as practiced in church.

Sunny and I and a group of other brash graduate students decided to organize our own "university" which initially met in a church. We would invite certain faculty to come down and talk to us. We studied all the ethical social codes since Hammurabi and tried to figure out how people organized to live together.[5] The professors thought our so-called "university" or "church" was intriguing. Many in our group went on to become professors themselves, including Urie Bronfenbrenner, who became the leading expert in the field of child development.[6]

One of our associates had volunteered with Friends Service Summer to build houses for miners in the Pittsburgh area.[7] This inspired our group of families to build our own houses on a tract of property we purchased outside of Ann Arbor. Sunny and I constructed our house out of cinder block – we have pictures of her doing masonry. Weekends and nights we would ride our bicycles out there and work until dark. We started in the summer, and by Christmas we were in.

Our daughter, Susan, and son, James, grew up in this five-family community, accepted by all the parents. I would say the best preparation for being a teacher is to raise your own kids – or try to. All the neighbor kids were in and about when I was trying to study for exams. If I'd have just thrown the books down and listened to them, I think I might have had a better sense of childhood and what was going on in their minds.

Sunny and women in our little community used to read about and discuss equality before Betty Friedan.[8] Sunny did a lot of community service and worked on political campaigns. The League of Women Voters was her life for quite a long time, and she was a local and state officer.[9] Sunny was an exceptionally good mother, with great empathy for children. I think it was due to her that our children never had the problems that were current at that time, such as drugs. They both turned out to be radical, but in ways we could approve. We admire their concern about people and the way they live their lives. Our children have adopted many of our values and both were trained as teachers. In later years, my son and I would build a cabin on a lake in Canada where we would spend our summers.

Albert Bandura says that fortuitous events have more to do with what happens in life than formal plans or normal processes.[10] One day, a professor told me, "Now, you've got to improve your writing, because as a PhD student ...." Well, I had no thought of that. He had taken it for granted that anybody enrolled in that advanced course was headed for a PhD. It was still the Depression, and there was a jobs program called NYA – National Youth Administration.[11] You could get paid 15 or 25 cents an hour working for a professor. So I joined the NYA and became a teaching fellow at the University of Michigan.

If you find one real mentor, I think you're lucky. But I had three. Professor Irving Anderson,[12] who had been trained at Harvard, brought a scientific perspective. When I began my thesis, not one sentence was good enough for him. I had been an English major and I thought I could write. Anderson taught me more rigorous thinking and scientific skepticism. Professor Howard McClusky[13] was very well read and a Renaissance man who crossed many disciplines and brought a humanistic perspective.

My most important mentor was Fritz Redl, a professor who came from Austria. I had been studying all this psychology and teaching educational psychology to teachers. But Fritz made psychology real, entirely different. I was his graduate assistant and we became very good friends. He was internationally renowned and yet unprofessorlike. Everybody called him Fritz, not "professor" or "doctor." He demonstrated total interpersonal democracy with colleagues. Remarkably, he would practice these same principles in work with disturbed and delinquent children at the University of Michigan Fresh Air Camp.

Chapter Two

Fresh Air Camp

One spring day, my dean asked me to ride with him through the hamlet of Hell, Michigan, to the University of Michigan Fresh Air Camp.[14] *So it came about that I began to work with children who were disturbed.*

In the early 1940s, I was a budding educational psychologist involved in opthalmologic research to discover how children read difficult material. In the summer, I brought my educational psychology classes to the University of Michigan Fresh Air Camp to hear this great man Fritz Redl. His insights really moved me. He was talking about things teachers need to know about real children.

Redl had been trained as a teacher in Austria by early pioneers who were applying psychoanalysis to education. He worked with August Aichhorn, who wrote *Wayward Youth,* and with Anna Freud.[15] It was apparent that it was not feasible to psychoanalyze all the kids, so the thing to do was to teach the teachers more about the nature of children. Fritz had been analyzed by Anna Freud but he never became doctrinaire.

As a young teacher, Redl had taken his kids out on the wanderlust, students and teachers exploring and camping together. He was deeply involved in activities with children. Other psychologists talked *about* the psychology of children, but I never saw the kids in their descriptions. Redl was so vivid and real. I would say to myself, "Yes, why didn't I see that?"

Redl was brought to the U.S. by the Progressive Educational Association which espoused John Dewey's philosophy of democracy in education.[16] He was a very broadly cultured person. His experiences as a teacher and psychologist in Austria gave him deep insights about disturbed kids. A colleague of mine said: "You should follow Fritz around with a bushel basket picking up the extra ideas he streams out. You only retrieve a little, there is so much."

Fritz had lived with children and didn't have to rely on books because he drew from direct experience. Fritz taught me about real children and how they thought and how they felt. That changed my direction again. A background in school psychology prepared me to sit in an office and test kids. But many were very difficult to test, which sparked my interest in clinical issues. My real experience was the University of Michigan Fresh Air Camp. Fritz had developed this therapeutic milieu program in a camp setting. We lived 24 hours a day with pre-adolescent and adolescent boys. Sometimes it seemed like 48 hours a day working with these very disturbed children who nobody knew how to manage.

Our research showed that there were three strengths that determined whether that kid was going to be able to make use of the camp setting: (1) be able to relate to adults; (2) be able to enjoy peer groups; and (3) find some enjoyment in the camping experience. If a youngster had two of these strengths, we could usually work successfully with him. With only one, the chances were slight. If he didn't have any, we shouldn't have taken him in the first place.

Camp was a strange culture for urban youth. Some who came from the center of Detroit would say, "How can you play ball, there are no streets." We studied their gang life and their group life. Peer groups, as Redl had shown us, became very important. I don't think my PhD helped me very much when I was invited to participate in school conferences on children in crisis. But direct experiences with such kids did. Teachers would say, "You must have been in my classroom." It was knowledge gained at the Fresh Air Camp.

I became convinced that you don't train teachers or other youth workers by the usual academic route. You need to be with them in a mentoring process. Teamwork is the core of training. Unless you work directly in the setting with the people who are trying to learn, and unless you can model these abilities, it doesn't count much. In order to teach them how to talk effectively with kids in crisis, you have to participate with them in the process.

Fritz left our University of Michigan camp and went to Wayne State University[17] in Detroit where he set up another camp of the same type. The university needed to replace Redl as director of their camp.

The University of Michigan Fresh Air Camp was located near a little town called Hell, Michigan. One day the dean said, "I want you to take a ride with me. Now, you can say you've been through hell with the dean." We went out and walked around the lake, the lodge, and the cabins. Finally, he said, "You're going to teach out here next summer." Well, I didn't have any options. But I was scared to death – going out there and running this camp for kids from the streets of Detroit.

The Fresh Air Camp idea was first established to bring poor kids from the city into the country so that they could breathe fresh air and be "fattened" up. They weighed them in and out in those days, and if a kid gained weight, it was considered a success. But the University of Michigan operated a very different kind of Fresh Air Camp. This was a training laboratory for professionals who aspired to work with disturbed and delinquent children and youth.

Graduate students were the camp counselors. At first, we brought them back to the University campus three days a week for classes. Then somebody got the bright idea of taking the training to them at the camp. Some professor would go out to the camp, teach a course, and then disappear back to campus. The students were having a good experience, but the classes were almost completely irrelevant. Except for Fritz, there was no relationship between what was dealt with in class and the experiences of these counselors.

For 15 years beginning in 1950, I was assigned the job of directing the camp. This meant raising the money, implementing a graduate educational program, and designing the program for campers. We ended up with education, psychology, and social work courses integrated with this field work. We also trained pediatricians, nurses, and teachers, in particular those entering the new field of special education for emotionally disturbed children.

We also had visiting professors from the related disciplines. Ralph Rabinovitch was our psychiatric consultant.[18] Child therapist Selma Fraiberg was on our staff.[19] Albert Cohen, who wrote about delinquent youth,[20] Bertram Cohler[21] and David Wineman[22] were faculty. We had a lot of visiting professionals including staff exchanges with Bruno Bettelheim's Orthogenic School in Chicago.[23]

In prior times, students might study Thrasher's *The Gang*,[24] ignoring the fact that you were working with an actual gang. The camp was a laboratory, and we traded formal course work for seminars on the camp milieu. Our educational program was built upon exploration of the clinical experience. We had a double staff so that one crew was in seminars or resting up while the other group was with the kids. We tried to create a therapeutic milieu following Redl and Wineman's ideas as described in their book, *The Aggressive Child*. We humanized the camping program, because rustic living can be a highly threatening and even punitive experience for kids from the inner city.

In the early days of camp, "muscle boys" taught various activities. We gradually got people who were more concerned about the kids than they were about who struck out in a baseball game. We tried to make the whole milieu foster mental health. That has been a theme of my life since that time. Properly designed, special education can be a more highly therapeutic experience for children than many formal "therapies."

Where is the dividing line between education and therapy? When does art become art therapy, and when does music become music therapy? Activities have psychological elements, but not always therapeutic. For instance, if you had some open paint buckets and brushes, how long is it going to be before disturbed kids will go wild?

Redl taught social ecology before the term was being used in psychology: the setting sucks out certain behavior. One night a week the cooks got off, so all the cabins had a cookout. I always ate early because that group activity produced contagion and chaos. Troubled kids building campfires in the woods? Also really stupid programming.

The role of the adult leader was very potent in the activities. When doing something they liked, such as crafts, the kids were always coming up and asking, "How do you do this?" The same leader who had been despised on the camp-out now became very prized and important. At the waterfront, kids called out, "See me swim; watch me swim" (even if they were walking on the bottom). Interactions between the adult and the child were highly influenced by the kind of activity. Certain activities could foster powerful therapeutic growth.

At Fresh Air Camp, we had "Drama Therapy" but never called it that. On one night of the week, all of the groups would put on a play. It was an enactment of what was going on in their lives, their families, their neighborhood. They loved to dress up like their parents. They would perform these dramas with aggressive, bombastic, disconnected episodes of violence. Some of the adults could not stand it because it got so rough.

Drama enables children to act out what is on their minds and in their feelings. We used these cathartic experiences as a springboard to discussion: "Why did your mother do that?" we asked. The child suddenly recognizes there must be some reason. "Well, maybe she was very tired because she'd been working so hard." By taking the role of the other person in a drama, they get a real sense of another's motivations.

Youth also respond to the beat, tempo, and lyrics of music. While I can't sympathize with some of the sounds of today, folk music is a universal expression. In every generation, the modern town crier makes the story into music. At camp, we played recorded stories over a loudspeaker. Tough kids would be sitting on the front steps of the lodge listening to a recording of the children's operetta, *Peter and the Wolf*.[25] Most of the time, they were raising hell, but here they are sitting and imagining, following that story and the threat of the wolf. Bruno Bettelheim's *The Uses of Enchantment* describes the meaning of fairy stories to children.[26] At such times of fantasy, the child is in his or her real world.

Research on the group psychology of games was initiated at the camp by Paul Gump and others.[27] If we tried to play baseball with these disturbed youngsters, by the time you got sides chosen, it was almost time to quit. Everybody wants to be batter and pitcher. Mistakes are magnified. A kid is out in the field, and the ball comes his way only once in the afternoon; then he misses it and is blamed for team failure. Baseball is a high threat game, but other activities have different properties. Tug of war is competitive, but individuals are not in the spotlight. No one has to be embarrassed by losing. "Maybe I pulled hard but the others didn't pull hard enough." This is a self-protective game. The right kinds of activities can be highly therapeutic for children in special education and other group settings.

Camp involved a week of pre-training and then eight weeks with children. Every kid came with a folder from the referral agency. Our application forms collected responses of kids themselves because the formal records didn't seem to tell much about how the youngster saw things. Traditional assessment doesn't tap the response of the child we are studying who gets lost in the paper shuffle.

David Wineman and I would assign campers to groups using available information. For instance, one kid is little but tougher than hell. If placed with his own age, he would dominate the group. But if "up-grouped" with older kids, they wouldn't be seduced by his behavior. He was no threat to them, just a little kid. If he swore at them, they wouldn't get upset. "So, what's with him?"

We learned quite a lot about the dynamics of grouping, and then the kids came. We would have an initial interview with each kid, and it was surprising how different the young person might appear from the case records. David would say, "My radar is lighting up," and we would have to regroup the youngster. He just would be a terror in the planned group, or conversely, another group would eat him up.

How much we learned in five minutes! A kid would strut in and say, "Where are the girls?" "Where do we smoke?" Their street sophistication might not match the records. Another kid would seem very vulnerable and in need of protection. We would shift our grouping depending upon what we thought the youngster needed. But once placed in a group, most did not want to get out, even if they were a scapegoat. That was their home no matter how they were treated. One camper was hiding under the porch, harassed by the others. He clearly was misgrouped, and I was trying to encourage him to move to another cabin where life would be better. But he would not even think about changing because it was a great defeat to be removed from his group.

The university camp was designed to provide support to kids in crisis as well as to the counselors. Staff worked as a team. When a counselor ran out of juice and couldn't figure what to do, one of us on the senior staff would sit down with the counselor and child and try to work out a solution. Rarely would we have to send a kid home or to the psychiatric hospital, less than one a year on average.

The limited data we had on counselors suggested that strengths some brought to this work were probably near zero. You could predict that some were going to have trouble while others seemed able to handle difficult kids. After we had worked with counselors for a week, we became much more cognizant of their strengths and limitations.

The camp ran on collaborative responsibility; it was democracy in action. No staff was alone, and there was always somebody to help. Of course, we didn't always solve the problem. The senior staff's responsibility was to come in when the group or individual situation got out of hand. We used strategies of "life space interviewing" that Redl and Wineman had pioneered.[28]

The life space interview is a planful problem-solving conversation between a young person and a responsible adult.[29] We want to know how the individual sees and thinks about an event. We neither talk *to* nor *at* a child, we talk *with* and interact. Once we are clear how a youngster perceives a problem we are in a position to work for a possible resolution. This approach is contrary to the stereotyped admonishing or threatening used by those in authority. It is also not like therapy based on interpretation, depth probing, or focus on the unconscious. Problems in the immediate life space became learning opportunities – both for the youngsters and the helping adult.

CHAPTER THREE

Troubled Students

The really impressive aspect is the investment of teachers in these children. It well may be that the nature of the interpersonal concern which they feel and express for these disturbed children is the major factor.[30]

Child guidance clinics were being established in the 1950s. The idea was, if you couldn't handle a child in school, refer him to the experts in the guidance clinic. Not much treatment was done by educators. If a student didn't fit, this was not seen as the job of the school. Let the clinic straighten him out and then send him back. It was in this era that many of the first specialized courses for teachers of disturbed or delinquent students began in Michigan universities.[31]

Teaching Teachers

When camp was over, I would return to the University in the fall as an instructor in educational psychology; it always seemed like a vacation. I didn't think the ordinary campus courses were very productive. The classes for future teachers were not related to the reality that they were going to face. Psychology, philosophy, and methods were disconnected, and it was up to the student to put them together. So I joined Max Wingo, an educational philosopher, and we team-taught aspiring teachers.[32]

I had been visiting schools in Ann Arbor and Livonia at the request of former students who would say, "Why don't you come out?" Teachers cannot be trained in isolation without contact with real kids in real educational situations. So teachers who had a difficult student would say, "Will you come out and talk about what we can do with this pupil?" Thus, "being there" became a professional theme for me.

I spent a day a week in the schools and was on call when we developed a teacher training program in the public schools. I was aiming for a replication of training at the Fresh Air Camp. In camp, I had both authority and responsibility, which was not the case in the public school. However, a small group of students stayed together for a year and we would meet in seminars.

When Ralph Rabinovitch came to the University of Michigan as director of the Children's Psychiatric Hospital,[33] he had a great belief in the therapeutic value of education. Instead, he found kids in the hospital's school were mostly reading comic books. They attended classes, but it was very permissive and not integrated with treatment. There was no curriculum, no bonafide school. Rabinovitch and I collaborated to make school a centerpiece of treatment.

Dr. R., as he was called, came out to camp and conducted our Friday night clinics. I developed a great respect for him, because he could spend an hour and find out more with a kid than we found out all week. Rabinovitch and his wife, Sara Dubo, also a child psychiatrist, worked as a team.[34] We were invited to send our students to the children's psychiatric hospital for internships.

In 1956, Michigan established Hawthorn Center,[35] a new psychiatric program and school for children and adolescents directed by Dr. Rabinovitch. This became a major site for our special education training program. I would go into the classes where my students were placed. As Hawthorn's educational consultant, once again I could integrate theory and practice as we had at Fresh Air Camp.

By then, Detroit had started public schools for emotionally and socially maladjusted students. Whether or not one called them "disturbed," most were usually delinquent and acting out. Few were "mentally retarded" since special classes were supposed to serve that population. In effect, these alternative programs served children and adolescents who were "school misfits."

Two kinds of people worked in these special schools which were increasingly common in big cities. One was the muscleman-coach type. Kids wouldn't openly misbehave because of the physical threat. Those teachers would say, "There isn't a kid in here that I can't lick." They bragged a lot about that. One said, "If I have any trouble, I bounce their heads off the blackboard." People of that demeanor were running classes for students who were very deprived and emotionally handicapped like our camp kids.

But there was another type of teacher in contrast to the strong-arm guys. These were devoted persons, often women, who were really able to connect with these children because of their love and caring. The kids sensed their desire to help. They were just wonderful people, most without much training, although some had courses in mental retardation. But they really cared about kids, and the kids responded. So you had the musclemen and the caring teachers in the same complex.

Most of these special schools had poor reputations. On the other hand, one had the best children's chorus in the city because there was a woman teacher who knew how to use music. She didn't call it music therapy; but she was doing therapy through music, building competence and self-esteem.

Around 1960, both Ann Arbor and Livonia[36] recognized a need for public classes for disturbed children. If a kid didn't make it at school, and a child guidance program couldn't cure him, then the only other option was institutionalization. There were no public school classes or therapeutic day schools at that time. Rabinovitch saw many kids referred to his center who didn't need residential placement. He thought that a lot could be done for these students in the public schools. He was a member of the Livonia school board which began to establish classes in the public schools for these disturbed youngsters.

Ann Arbor also started special classes. Students in these suburban settings were not particularly violent like we see so often today. They were a mixed bag of LD and psychiatric cases. There was not too much concern about diagnosis. A school psychologist simply decided this is a kid who needed this help. If outpatient treatment in a child guidance clinic was not enough, then the school would provide special classes. If they could not be managed and taught in school, the next step was a residential placement.

There were great debates about how these early classes should be conducted. Before behavioral approaches, Freudian theory dominated.

That was a period of "let the poison out." Teachers were not supposed to do "therapy." They were to teach these youngsters, but it was to be in a permissive environment. They tried to develop relationships with these disturbed kids mostly from middle class families as in Ann Arbor and Livonia. Of course, there were aggressive kids in the bunch, but it was not the main pathology like we are dealing with now.

A New Kind of Student

When special education for troubled students was established under Public Law 94-142, children with "serious emotional disturbance" were among the categories of handicapped students entitled to an education. But it was very clear that this was *not* a mental health initiative. It is an educational law and takes quite a conservative educational view. It leaves out many disturbed youngsters, particularly those arbitrarily designated as "socially maladjusted."

Subsequently, there was a great effort to change the legal definition of serious emotional disturbance. The Council for Children with Behavioral Disorders[37] wanted a simple but more inclusive definition, a well-meaning but impossible wish. The original definition was copied from Eli Bower, who had studied emotionally handicapped students in California.[38] His research described specific patterns of behavior which included both socially and emotionally handicapped children. This inclusive definition never became law. Of course, special education has never been comfortable with delinquents in the first place. So those who don't know what to do with that half of the disturbed population conveniently shift them to another category. Thus began the effort to separate those who "deserved" special education from those who would be police responsibility. While the federal definition of serious emotional disturbance was woefully inadequate, no one could propose a politically acceptable alternative.

When I was working with Hawthorn Center, a mental health team went to juvenile delinquency facilities to find out how many kids really were emotionally disturbed, even though they were classed as only social delinquents. As if you could separate. But the team wanted to know how many students were entitled to special education even under restrictive current laws. They found that between 30 and 40 percent of these delinquent students should have qualified for special education and related mental health services. But they were treated as just plain delinquents.

Society faces a new type of challenge: kids who do not have pro-social values. They have values, but these are not values that we can live with in society. There's an article someplace in *Ortho*[39] about boys ages seven, eight, or nine who have murdered somebody. The authors asked them about what their biggest problem is. Remember, they have just killed somebody. They say, "Well, my biggest problem is I don't read good" or something just as unrelated. They have no feeling for anybody else and get kicked out of school for hurting other people. Nowadays, girls are beginning to match boys in aggressiveness.

All this balderdash that "socially maladjusted" students should not be in special classes is nonsense. They always were and always will be the biggest problem schools face. A nice withdrawn student sits in the corner and does his work and just dreams or wanders around. That kid can be tolerated in the mainstream (though it may offer no help). More and more extremely aggressive kids have been seriously damaged by violence in the home and neighborhood. Many are abused kids without a sense of their identity and with no models of reasonable adult behavior. These are the kind of kids we're getting now, given the disintegration of child raising today.

These tremendous social problems will not be cured by more special education. In some communities, half the kids are at risk. The whole system needs redesign. We cannot just funnel a few kids off to special education. In the past, a school psychologist, clinical psychologist, or rarely a child psychiatrist was called in to "certify" many cases. That was unfortunate because many clinicians really didn't know beans about these kids but were supposed to be the gatekeepers.

Psychologists and psychiatrists are generally more interested in diagnosis than prognosis. They document what the child is like currently. Schools want to know, "What hope is there for this pupil?" While we need diagnosis, we have not paid enough attention to prognosis. The pay-off of assessment for a teacher is: "What can I hope for this child, and how do I help?" Too many teachers have to make their own prognosis. Some are discouraged about the future of a pupil when they shouldn't be. Others have naïve hope, neglecting the depth of damage.

The common concern is "How long do we keep them in special education?" In Ann Arbor the answer was "one year and out." Some were kept much longer but still weren't ready for the mainstream. There was little to support them when they returned. In the heyday of child guidance, the notion was, "Cure them and send them back." Now it became, "Fix them in special classes and then maybe we'll take them back." Of course, regular schools were in no hurry to take them back since the reputations of these kids were notorious.

We also don't pay much attention to the depressed kids whose needs are less obvious than those who act out. In the early days, we wanted to get help for a depressed sour apple and a sad apple. But seldom now; those kids just sit there. We need prevention and mental health programs for the average kid. But the psychologists and social workers who used to enrich the quality of the school experience for all children are busy testing and filing papers.

So, current society is producing a different kind of pathology. How will we respond to these new challenges? Many say that we should not be wasting resources on socially maladjusted students. I'm always interested in efforts to limit who deserves help. It irritates me that anyone would think we shouldn't help children because they have a value deficit problem. Who needs more help than these kids, if for no other reason but our own self-preservation?

Families on the Edge

Today, many families are in crisis, but they too must have pretty severe problems to get special help. All programs give lip service to working with parents, but it is not so easy. Some families face outright survival problems so the child's difficulty is incidental to their life dilemma. Middle class parents may not be preoccupied with survival, but the disturbed child is an embarrassment and disgrace. Families see their problems quite differently than do professionals.

Even if the family shows up for conferences, not much may be accomplished. For schools and mental health workers to involve families in the most serious cases is a very difficult challenge. We should do everything we can to provide normal family opportunities, but this is sometimes not possible. Even if a child is placed in a foster home, that can also be a tragedy. The hard reality is that the ecology resists significant change, and some of these young persons are going to have to save themselves.

We fail to recognize the dollar expense of massive social change. Society once had a lot of free help for raising kids – it was called the family. Mothers donated their lives to raising children. That free child-raising function has been replaced by baby care, preschool, and after-school programs. But, we're paying a bigger financial and psychological cost. It is very difficult to get the quality of relationships that a concerned family can offer. I've had kids tell me, "You're just listening to me because you're paid for it." They want to feel that they're accepted by a caring adult, not as a cash exchange.

Someone has said that the greatest distance between two people is the space between a parent and a child. But this should be as close as any two human beings can be. Yet some children are raised in "pseudo-families" where parenting has never functioned properly. Thus, teachers may have to teach values, not just supplement them from home. We have to teach them who they are and that they are worthwhile. They need to learn how to relate to people, particularly the adults in authority. This change has not been recognized in schools, which are ill equipped to be surrogate families to psychological orphans. Schooling remains an assembly line knowledge factory.

Many parents of emotionally disturbed kids remember their own poor experience in school. They have a hard time realizing this teacher isn't the enemy they remember. Most families are concerned about what happens in school. But parents bring their biases and kids bring their tales, so communication can easily be distorted.

Good schools enlist parents as partners and advocates for their children. One mother who learned that authorities were considering cutting a program for disturbed students said, "I just hope they won't do it. That's the only school experience he has where they haven't sent him home or called up and had a negative kind of 'conference'. I'm so glad. I'm not afraid of the phone ringing anymore."

We started an organization for parents of emotionally disturbed children, MAEDC, as an alliance between families and professionals.[40] Parents became very active in lobbying. In Ann Arbor, we had a local advisory board of parents for the special education program. We sat down with teachers to consider the needs of pupils in a high problem school. Then the group decided to develop a proposal to the state about the kind of professional services and programs required to provide both academic and mental health support for *all* children. These changes would not increase costs as they would be keyed to the existing school budget. Basically, parents and teachers would decide what resources they wanted to have. For example, perhaps this would mean more (or fewer) psychologists. Furthermore, this parent/professional group would tell the special personnel what services were needed. So it wasn't like each specialist coming in with a pre-set role to enact in the school.

We thought it was a pretty exciting idea and parents from all the different special education categories came on board. But outside special interest groups didn't like the precedent of putting earmarked funds in a general pot. And, psychologists also were resistant since they might be asked to fill a different role. The same thing was apparent with the other special education disciplines. All of this was highly threatening. We spent two years on this proposal and developed a healthy respect for how hard it is to change systems.

Listening to Consumers

Broad efforts to establish special classes for emotionally disturbed children began in the late 1950s. We thought we were doing holy work at that time. These kids who were kicked out of regular classes were sitting in the office half the time, their lives were quite miserable. Some were depressed, and teachers wanted help for them. So we began to develop special classes for kids with emotional problems and tried to get them mental health services. We felt so good about ourselves: "Look what we are doing!" Nowadays, they tell us we were evil, and the classes were a curse. We saw ourselves as great helpers, yet the kids we were trying to help often didn't find the classes helpful at all.

There has always been a wide gulf between perceptions of the pupil and parent consumers and the special educators. Until required by law, we didn't listen to parents much, although if they raised hell, their child might not be put in special classes. But when the school decided this was where the student should go, there was often very little conversation. Parents were "notified" about the action. We didn't share test information. We did little to help parents understand the decision, and even less for the pupil. In fact, we had many stratagems to prevent parents from participating with us in the life of the child.

A lot of these kids came from families in great turmoil, so the simplistic solution was to refer both the child and parent for therapy. Many times, the ineffectiveness of traditional therapy provided for these families and children was obvious. The kids were supposed to be cured and go back to regular classes, but many couldn't make it. Somehow the whole thing didn't seem right.

The Council for Exceptional Children (CEC) recognized the problems in this area of special education and proposed a study of programs. I joined with Richard Cutler and Albert Fink to conduct this first national study.[41] There were many different approaches in these various programs for disturbed children. The quality ranged from a near madhouse where "therapeutic" chaos reigned, to rigid, silent seat-sitting morgues. Remarkably there were many teachers who developed their own styles which were a clear benefit to distraught students.[42]

This was a real eye-opener, and such research has been repeated in different forms in subsequent decades.[43] Unfortunately, little has changed except the basic theory for managing these kids. Instead of psychodynamics, we now have behavior modification. Knitzer's study called typical programs *curriculums of control*.[44]

Our early study collected data from teachers, administrators, and children, and by direct observation in field visits. The emphasis on getting data directly from the kid consumers has remained very important for me. The main goal of special classes was to get troubled kids out of the hair of the regular system. Possible benefits to students were incidental. These were kids who fouled the nest and schools wanted them removed. If you can find a teacher who can live with them, fine, as long as they don't disturb the rest of the school. Classes were sometimes exiled to the basement to get them out of sight.

We thought we were doing noble work. But when you would talk to the children about their experience, you'd get a very different picture. Many students hated being placed among other outcasts. The motivation of a pupil is so important, but too often we don't really talk enough about that. In their view, we are saying, "You are now going to be in this class as punishment for your sins, and a special bus will pick you up."

For some children, this was the first time they could survive in school and the special class was an oasis. In one school, a kid we will call Carl asked the special education teacher to let him in her class. The teacher said, "You can't just walk in. You've got to go through the process to get in." She explained all the required rituals for partaking of the "holy mass." It was very funny. Carl said, "I think I should, I wanna be in here. You only have 10 kids; you can take one more kid." Carl was having such a bad time; he knew that he wasn't going to make it in regular education. He said, "Look, I've been kicked out so many times, and this is my last chance." He did get in the class, and he was highly motivated to succeed, but this was a threat to others in the special class.

These were recalcitrant, delinquent adolescents with no commitment to learn. They had been forced to be in this class. But Carl chose to be here so he would do his work. Kids have their own DSM[45] system and radar for kinship. They could sense that Carl shared their troubled background, but he didn't behave like them: He cooperated with the teacher whom they saw as the enemy. So they started working him over. "Look at this kid doing this dumb work." They tried to destroy his personal motivation.

Carl took it for a while, and finally he let them have it, threatening them. Using language they recognized, he said, "You let me alone or I'm gonna beat the _____ out of you. This is my last chance, and you guys aren't gonna make me lose it." The peers went into shock. They couldn't understand why a kid like them was trying to use the special class.

Schools have been obligated since Public Law 94-142[46] to educate emotionally disturbed children. Many of these kids need treatment services, but mental health has no legal mandate to help in school. The way mental health is traditionally practiced isn't going to be too helpful anyway. Some experts say that if education joins with mental health, a solution would be found. But, unless schools and mental health both change, we are in a bind. Programs for this population are the least effective in special education. We need fresh ways to look at these children and positive strategies to meet their diverse needs.

CHAPTER FOUR

Deviance or Variance?

What we think works constitutes the theory behind our practice.
Recognized or not, each one of us has a theory of human nature.[47]

It's very hard to sustain a positive ethos with kids in conflict because fundamentally what we want to do to fix up kids is to punish them into goodness. If Redl did anything, he talked about the impossibility of using punishment as a major motif of child rearing. That's where the clash with behaviorism came. Most of the early primitive behaviorists put us back years in thinking about how to deal with disturbed youngsters. But the school welcomed it because it fit the ideology of control. When our theories don't fit the needs of children, this is a tragedy.

Theory Wars

Many different models have been put forth to explain problem behavior. Bill Rhodes[48] was at the University of Michigan in Ann Arbor when he finished his study of major theories of children's behavior disorders, which he called "child variance." A colleague, Judith N. Smith[49] suggested we convert the theories into videotapes of problem classroom behavior to use in training teachers. We got a bunch of kids and a great director to help us portray classroom discipline problems. The kids were normal students who were to enact certain scenes, not as scripted but just as a setting for spontaneous reactions on their part. These incidents were then to be analyzed by experts from different theoretical points of view.[50]

One of the fascinating things was how good the kids were at acting "bad." The film director would describe the scenario to the youth.

"Okay, you're going to bug the teacher." Or "Here's a kid who acts like so." We'd set a loose frame of reference and leave it to their creativity. These kids really fell into the dramatic format and loved it. They were being photographed doing bad things, but since they had "permission," no guilt. Some scenes came close to reality.

The videos simulated small classes of students, and those acting as the teacher were actual special education professionals who work with emotionally troubled students. However, the teacher actors did not know what the kids were going to do. We wanted them to struggle and be spontaneous in order to develop the dramatic scene. One teacher told me afterwards, "I'd never do that again." Since she didn't know these kids, she could not make informed responses, which is one of the problems with the whole project. While the teachers did a lot of stupid things, the tapes are good stimuli for discussion, but they hardly present adequate classroom images.

These vignettes depicted different kinds of child behavior problems in school. Since most problems were just extensions of the child actor's own experience, they had no problem bugging a teacher or bullying a peer. They were less confident portraying an autistic youngster since such behavior was foreign to them. Isn't the behavior of disturbed kids just the extension of the normal distribution? That is why we used the term "variance" instead of disorders.

After the scenes were filmed, we scoured the country to find experts to represent different theories of behavior. We would put at least two of these people with contrasting views together for a session. After viewing a particular vignette, each would discuss how they would handle that situation from their theoretic perspective. Most experts wanted to know more about the case and situation. As they gave their supposedly specialized advice, it got kind of homogenized. It was as if "I'm a great behaviorist, but here I'm not so sure." Tidy theories tended to melt around the edges. You could put a rabble-rousing advocate of one persuasion with some contrary expert. Viewing the same problem, they frequently were not that different.

When teachers looked at the films of the national experts, they would often say, "Good God, I've got better ideas than that." It elevated the teachers' sense of professional self-efficacy. In spite of all their publications, the experts didn't know that much more about what was appropriate in the actual situation.

Looking back, I think the project was ill-conceived. Talking about philosophies may be appropriate in a graduate seminar for people who like to play with theory. But if I'm going to meet a class tomorrow, I don't think that's the right way to prepare.

Theories somehow narrow the vision. Albert Bandura once said that if the human organism was like some of the radical behaviorists believe, the species would have died out generations ago. You find what you look for, and a narrow view tends to distort the subject.

Destructive Values

Many systems for troubled children are too mechanical and superficial. If a youth doesn't give a damn about anybody or feels so maligned that the only way to survive is by exploiting those around him – until those values are changed, all your interventions do is to make the kid more sophisticated in pathological behavior. So I believe that our aim ultimately should be much deeper change.

Our challenge with youth today is not so much to clarify values but to change them. Schools used to get kids who were mostly oriented to responsible values. Now, many embrace beliefs alien to the society we are trying to build. Even delinquent kids have a value system: "If you can get away with it, do it." These destructive values are often modeled by the media or older peers.

Values are learned through the processes of identification. For instance, youth who do not have any role models to demonstrate a good work ethic will have difficulty in employment. Likewise, if parents have no respect for schooling, the kid has no models for achievement. When a kid comes home, do parents ask, "What did you do in school today?" Or do they look at the school books and say, "You're still studying that crap?" Without a positive model for learning and social behavior, the child is adrift.

Materialistic cultural values add to the problem. Frankly, if you can make the money some of these kids make peddling drugs, it is pretty difficult in a money-oriented economy to tell them, "That's a bad thing to do." They see this hypocrisy all around in the adult society. Self-centered behavior and thinking will only change because of a cardinal value that we care for one another and won't hurt each other.

Most schools don't shape core values. Educators seldom get far enough into the child's inner life to make a real difference. The school tries to stomp out problem behavior with superficial interventions. But kids do not change because of verbalisms or virtue posters. It is a myth that one builds character with videos and moral platitudes. Deep values cannot be taught by little lessons in "let's say please."

Nicholas Hobbs challenged educators to use group processes to build positive behavior.[51] To make lasting changes in behavior, one must enlist peers because they have so much influence on one another. For example, if a kid has been ostracized by a group, acceptance requires changes in peers as well as in the youngster. Just telling him to be nice, not to swear, and not to fight isn't enough. We need to change the peer culture. The child has to try new behavior and involve the group in discussing the results.

Values are learned in real-world encounters. One time I was visiting a program in Brooklyn and kids were discussing what to do if a clerk gives back too much change. What had happened is they'd gone to a store with a one dollar bill – that rarity of all rarities happened – the guy gave them change as if it was a five. They were hilarious after they got out of the store. They came to class, and told the teacher, "Well, you know that dumb bastard gave us …"

In their initial discussion, the teacher avoided moralizing. The idea that they shouldn't have kept the money came up in the conversation, but others felt this was justice done for prior wrongs to them. The students asked the teacher, "What would you do?" Then he had to explain his own values; they really put him on the hot seat. He said, "I'll tell you, first of all, I have an approach when I go into a store because it usually happens the other way." He knows the kids claim that "We always get shortchanged, this is just payback, it's fair." The teacher said, "When I give a clerk a large bill, I always announce what it is, like 'Here is ten dollars.' I make a point of that so that I don't get into these situations. Then I don't get cheated like you've been cheated. So I don't have any reason to cheat them."

The deepest conversations we can have with youth are about values, which is why I don't like canned programs. I was working with a group of young teens and the topic of sex came up. They said that they never talked about things that are important to them in school. I said, "Well, what would you say if we see if we can get a course on that." They said, "Oh my God! No! When the school gets it, it dies." Even something as potentially interesting as sex education would fail when it becomes a course. So, we decided to have a group meeting on such issues *after* school. Our best avenue to reach today's adolescents, as Hobbs says, is through the group process.

Diverse Needs

School is designed for a fabricated average-for-age normal child who never existed. When you tell a junior high or a sixth grade teacher, "You know, you're teaching all grades in a one-room school," they look at you like you are crazy. If you look at the actual range of achievement which increases with every grade, there are some non-readers; there are some kids who probably are way up in the 10th grade. This is an expanded one-room school but teaching is to a mythical average, though it may fit no one in the group. This is the challenge of accommodating individual differences in children.

It is a very complex task to restructure schools to accommodate childhood variance. Whenever we can meet the needs of the special child in regular classes, we can have inclusion. But the standard for main-streaming is that the student is *surviving* in a regular class. These students may have no friends, may be unable to do the work, and may have terrible feelings about themselves. Survival is not enough; the goal should be *thriving*. If needs are not met in a regular class or cannot be met for whatever reasons, then children need a more enriched setting. Not all types of handicaps are equally easy to accommodate, and studies show emotionally disturbed students are the hardest. Whether the kid thinks school is good or bad for him may be the essential point.

Gender creates another important variance. Programs for troubled students have been dominated by boys but girls are fast catching up. Eleanor Maccoby's study on sex differences showed that aggression loaded on the male side.[52] Actually, I don't think girls are less aggressive; instead, they use a different style of aggression. Likewise, middle class people are aggressive, but they do it in a way that I'm used to. I don't have the same sense of being aggressed upon that I would if they had hit me in the face. With greater equality of the sexes, each gender behaves more like the other and more girls are referred for problems.

The system also responds to girls in a different fashion than boys. In general, girls have to be very bad before they get referred. Many have been overlooked along the way, especially if they have not acted out. Rabinovitch made a study of this at Hawthorn Center. He found that kids are placed not because of the depth of pathology but when the environment has exhausted the toleration for the behavior. The home, school, or community just cannot stand it anymore. Some kids were brought at midnight in handcuffs by the police out to that mental health facility. The reason, when you trace it back, was that the parents couldn't any longer tolerate the behavior and had no means of handling the kid.

Many acting-out kids are really defensively displaying their depression. Depressed girls are often ignored until they try suicide or something drastic. The system is so focused on responding to aggression that the quiet pathologies are overlooked. Kids do not qualify for services as emotionally disturbed unless their problems interfere with school performance. Schools can endure an autistic child sitting isolated in a class much better than a kid who sneers, defies, and destroys the motivation of other students. We cannot tolerate a child who "contages" his peers to behave against the system.

Children also vary in their capacity to use a therapeutic environment. Some exploit our benevolence and misuse a benign milieu. They may need to be brought into reality by clearly seeing what the alternatives are. I used to employ the "reality principle." Children whose behavior is putting them on the brink need to recognize how precarious their situation is and what the actual choices are. We might tell a youngster that the next time this happens, this is the only thing we can figure to do: your mother's got to come in here and go over things, your father's got to come in, you're going to have to go and see somebody about your problem. When we start talking realistically, often the kid finds new inner resources. We help by highlighting reality.

All of this reflects a basic theme: *we have to pay a lot more attention to the youngster.* This big bureaucratic system may be oblivious about what is going on in the mind of a kid. For instance, you ask, "How did you get in this special class?" the response is, "Well, I went to see that man," or "I met with that lady and we played them 'games,'" or "I saw the psychologist and the next thing I know they sent me here." We may say this kid needs therapy but don't have a clue about his or her world-view. Unless the young person sees our attempts to help as useful, our interventions are not going to be very productive.

CHAPTER FIVE

Connecting in Crisis

All behavior makes sense if we could but
understand the meaning to the person performing it.

The foundation for all work with youth is to understand how one person helps another. We start by exploring our own naïve theories of behavior. To whom or what do we attribute the problems kids display? How much do we fault them? Do we blame society? Biology? Cursedness? These deep private beliefs hardly even surface in the training or research literature. I've heard teachers say to students, "Well, nobody can help you. You've got to help yourself." Well, it's true, but it's untrue. We've got to help them. Together – we have got to do it. While some helpers are pessimists, others operate on the illusion that they are going to accomplish miracles and cure the child.

When Bill Rhodes was at the University of Michigan, he influenced me to read *If You Meet the Buddha on the Road, Kill Him* where the nature of helping is vividly portrayed.[53] Effective helpers empathize with a child in his or her dilemma. Children also want to know about the helper. Frequently, they ask us questions about your own life. You're not supposed to talk about that. You're supposed to keep your distance. But I don't think that's right at all. Basically, to be a helper you have to engage in the exploration of life, and you begin by understanding your own life.

Children know how to push our buttons. One time at camp, the kids were teasing me and trying to get my goat. I had a day off and was sailing my boat when the wind went down. I was just sitting there, dead in the water. So they rowed out by me and started calling me names like "dummy" and less quotable. "See, you can't go anyplace." After a while, I said, "You know, I'm liable to get mad." In all seriousness, one boy said, "You can't get mad. You're supposed to be in charge of this place." You're not allowed to get mad was what he was telling me. They acted shocked. I was from a different world with different rules.

When I would have a group session with these kids, it could get very rough. Once, to get the attention of an out-of-control group, I pounded on the table and said, "Damn it, shut up!" They looked very holy and shocked, "What you said?" They'd just been swearing a blue streak. I said, "Damn it, shut up," and that was a big crime on my part. We talked about how I had the same feelings that they had. I have the same problems of control that they do because we are all human beings. "You are really bugging me. You are trying to get me mad. I know what you are doing, and maybe even why." As I share my human experience, and as I can make connections with other people's human experience, I might be able to help.

A lot of us would not be able to cope with the lives many disturbed children face day by day. I see youngsters punished and berated for their misbehavior as if adults were perfect. One kid said, "I'm in this program because I had all kinds of problems. Then when I have a problem, they have a fit about it. I thought this was where you come to get help with your problems." What they see going on is not what I might think as an adult. The adult helping fantasy is I'm in holy work, helping distraught children; we are so preoccupied with ourselves, we don't see the world from the child's point of view.

In 1965, we published the first of many editions of *Conflict in the Classroom*[54] (Nick Long, Ruth Newman, and I). That book used stories to teach what it is like to be a disturbed child. Some selections were autobiographical, others creative literature. People have told us that they get more out of the stories than all of the academic sections.

Adults need to relearn how children look at life from the knee-high point of view. I have a collection of books from the child's viewpoint – one aptly titled *Life Among the Giants*.[55] Children do not study us formally, but they seem to understand a whole lot of what's going on with adults. Kids get bossed around from every angle and told what to do. They become better psychologists than we are because they have to survive with our peculiar ways and our domination. We can never return to their world; but to understand children, we have to listen to their messages with empathy.

A Crisis Teacher

In Ann Arbor, the teachers said, "We don't have the kind of worker we ought to have in schools." "So what kind of worker should you have?" we asked. They said, "We don't need more guys like you." They were gentle about it, but that's what they said. Not more psychologists and their rituals. We need a teacher who also can deal with these kids at the times schools cannot handle them. In these moments of crisis, they need skilled helpers to deal with emotions and teach new skills. Most unmanageable pupils act that way episodically and don't need full time exclusion. That is where crisis intervention is needed.

We always had full-time crisis support persons in camp, so it seemed sensible to do the same in schools. But these teachers had come to their own independent conclusion. Actually, the kinds of people we are talking about are called educational therapists in California. They have specialized training and have established the Association of Educational Therapists.[56] Those are people who know how to teach the basic academic skills but who are also therapeutically oriented.

The teachers told us they wanted a teacher who could sit down with these kids around the problem the child was having in class – whether it be general behavior or behavior due to frustration in the tasks or academics. This teacher would be free of class responsibility. That would be more important to teachers than all the other outside specialists and classes that take the child away and never meet the need. The crisis teacher offers an entirely new format for learning when classroom progress is interrupted by behavior or academic frustration. Needs are addressed but not by punishment in the principal's office.

Our first crisis teacher was just an ace, a real Jewish mother type in the best sense. She could do things with those kids that none of the rest of us could imagine. As we expanded to other schools, I learned another lesson: the idea was no better than the agent. Some people were good, but some were lousy. Often they were punitive instead of therapeutic. They would not give up their rigid rituals of education.

To teach disturbed kids or deal with their crises, you have to be half mental health and half education. The trouble with mental health people in schools is that they are not half education. Few really appreciate what it means to deal with a group of these kids. They will give advice about what the teacher ought to do that's complete nonsense, given the number of kids they have to manage. Blending teaching and therapy isn't simple.

There have been ongoing debates between advocates for discipline versus mental health. We found that mental health folks have to be "disciplinarians" in the best sense. They can't ignore reality and consequences but have to be tough-minded, which many of the profession are not. The principal also needs mental health skills in order to discover the real problem. Often by the time someone in authority was available, the kid had forgotten all about the event. Then the adult spent time reminding him of how bad he was.

As more and more disturbed children are integrated in the mainstream, we will need to have more crisis intervention. Schools can use a lot of psychological help. One trouble is the specialists may spend more time running from school to school in their cars than they do in the schools. Crisis intervention requires a person stationed in the schools, not itinerant. In times of crisis, students open up to depths not otherwise accessible.

Kids in Pain

Just because a youth displays aggressive behavior does not necessarily mean he or she lacks positive qualities. These are children expressing deep pain. I remember a little red-headed boy at Fresh Air Camp who had a terrible temper. He had been creating havoc after bedtime, and I had to physically carry him out of the cabin. He got so anxious at night because his dreams were so bad that he was afraid to sleep. So he raised hell every evening when it was time for taps. Getting a group of eight kids in a cabin quieted down is an enterprise, and this kid kept the place in an uproar. So I was removing him from the group to calm him down.

As I carried him out, he was screaming and biting. When he calmed down, he said: "The trouble is my goddamn temper. I got this red hair. I got this temper." He had probably been told this many times. And he added, "If I could only control this temper, things wouldn't be like this."

He wanted to be a better kid; he had the goal and the desire. He just didn't know how to handle his impulses. Then he shared what was bothering him. "You know, I don't know who my real father and mother are. My family adopted me. They think I don't know I'm adopted, but I heard them talking one time. If you don't know who your parents are, how do you know who you're gonna be like?" His whole inner turmoil spilled out in a torrent.

In a moment of crisis, you can discover the inner child. The boy's red hair was not his problem. His wild bedtime behavior was not his problem. His values were not his problem. What was bothering him was, "I don't know who I am." He was flooded with questions like, "Why did my parents desert me? Wasn't I worth being taken care of?" No wonder he was afraid of being alone with his thoughts in the night.

The reason I can empathize with a child and form a helping alliance is that the person has shared a piece of his life. So I think we are going to get more progress in humanizing the school by changing it from a bureaucratic to a more personal, problem-solving orientation. As adults learn how to talk with children and better understand them, how to use the crises to explore the nature of a child, there will grow a new level of mutual attachment. I cannot approach the youngster the same way tomorrow as I did yesterday with what I now know.

Being with a youth in crisis is a primary interpersonal experience. The child remembers this important moment. And, what I read in a case record doesn't have the impact as when this child has shared this problem with me. Of course, the child who has let you into his or her life expects you to do something about it. That may be why we don't want to get involved, because of the responsibility to help.

When I communicate with a child about some important aspect of life, we become more significant persons to one another. That doesn't mean that it's going to be easy or comfortable. But it means that I now understand that child better and therefore can't be as unforgiving and as crass as I might have been yesterday. So I think the change in school is going back to some of the early ideas from the child study movement, rather than depending only on administrative fiats and test scores for a revolution in education.

CHAPTER SIX

Working with Groups

The group's power is derived in part from contagion of spirit.
Contagion can sweep over a group and move it to enthusiasm or hostility.[57]

Many mental health professionals don't understand that the teacher is primarily a group worker. While teachers also lack training in group dynamics, they constantly work with groups of children. Many disturbed kids do best in a one-to-one situation, but schools are not organized this way. Further, teachers often experience groups of youth as adversaries rather than allies. There is no professional task more taxing than teaching a group of contrary, troubled youngsters.

Teachers and other group workers play many different roles which contribute to group problems. One moment you are helping a student with schoolwork. The next minute, some kid goes by and kicks the student, who blows his stack. One has to be a tutor, policeman, lawyer, and surrogate parent. But there are no formal procedures for role switching. Nobody says, "Now I'm going to be this" or "Now's the time to be that." As situations change, we need to instantaneously adapt.

Kids have trouble keeping our roles straight. For example, campers would complain about their terrible counselor when actually she was the most loving, wonderful person you could ever wish to see. I would ask them, "How do you decide she is terrible?" They would tell me about some little thing that happened. They would blame everything on that non-consequential incident. They had made her into such a perfect person that any imperfection became magnified. She was such a wonderful person that they were being challenged by her to look at adults in a different way. It was very hard for them. Their opposition to adults as unhelpful was being challenged. They couldn't manage this. Shifting adult-child roles requires a considerable amount of subtlety and management.

Kids have all kinds of games they play on us to see if they can bring us down to their level. One favorite is the "You're not fair" game. That game gets to almost any of us who aspire to be fair. They tell me I'm not fair, and the next thing I know, I'm defending myself: I am too fair and it's not fair for you to say I'm not. Another game is the comparative anthropologist game. "My other staff says…" They are carefully studying us and pitting us against one another. Emotionally disturbed students have not had good past experiences with adults and so learn to be skillful manipulators to protect their interests.

Group Contagion

Groups of disturbed children tend to produce contagion, said Redl. Somebody drops a pencil, and pretty soon a lot of pencils drop. This rapid-fire modeling spirals to the point where the whole group gets infected. It is important to discover what roles particular individuals play in this group process.

There is frequently a provocateur in the contagion episodes, a kid who leads. For instance, the assigned work looks hard and it is not exciting. So, one skillful manipulator might say something to prompt others who are less astute into a rebellion. "Do we have to do all of this? All 20 pages?" His innocent question sparks feelings of opposition in the group. Another youth, who wouldn't have said anything, is now given bravado to boldly confront the teacher with no hesitation or guilt. So the upward spiral starts, and soon everyone believes the teacher is unfair. You can see it developing. It is going to disintegrate the whole process if you don't stop it.

If you are lucky, when contagion goes too far, it can self-correct. For instance, one time I was walking in the hall at school and met a teacher who was obviously distraught. I said, "What happened?" She said, "I can't stand it anymore in that class. They're just bugging the life out of me – I didn't want to break down and cry – and I didn't want to shout at them. So I just got out." As we stood talking about this group and its mass contagion, a student came up to her and said, "You can come back now. It's going to be all right."

What had happened is what Redl called "shock." As the behavior got wilder and wilder, some of the kids began to get anxious. Now anxiety in some disturbed kids may only increase their acting out. But there are others who may want to separate themselves from this behavior. In their minds, it is all right to bother the teacher, but you shouldn't drive her out. Their reservations may result from empathy or fear of consequence.

The process of shock works like this. The leader of the contagion brags, "We got rid of two other teachers. Let's get rid of her, too." But some of the more sensible kids start thinking: "Three teachers out, my God, what's going to happen to us? Anyway she's a nice person – we shouldn't pick on her." The mass contagion begins to melt as the leader loses his following because of "shock" in a group.

Sometimes the group may even turn against the provocateur who's been leading them astray. They begin to scapegoat their former leader. "Look what you did!" They are thinking, of course, we did stuff, too, but we didn't do anything like you did. Our sins are so minor compared to yours. You actually swore at her. In this interesting reversal of the direction of contagion, the leader becomes *persona non grata*. The group changes its values as members become holy and project the badness onto this one person.

In some groups, there is nobody whose conscience gets alerted by the anxiety produced by the behavior. Rather than stop, they escalate out of control. This is common in very young children who have not yet developed much self-control. They just go wild every once in a while. In a group of kindergarten kids, somebody starts running around and yelling. Pretty soon the whole group follows like a flock and they are all just wild.

Another type of contagion involves two or more pupils who share the same pathology. Perhaps it is a sexual problem – so any innocent comment becomes sexualized. With some preadolescents anything can have a sexual connotation. They match Freud. If the teacher talks to one about an inappropriate remark, others start giggling all over the room. Then if one tries to confront this contagion, children act innocent. Kids will say, "Don't you want me to be happy?" They'd say, "Can't you enjoy life? I'm giggling, I'm having a good time." Instant communication seems to connect students with similar pathologies.

In a group of problem students, many share the same problems: (1) I'm not good in school; (2) I've had a bad time with women; (3) I've got a sexual problem; and (4) I also have very low self-esteem. If something happens to trigger one of these problems, it can quickly set off others in the group. What starts out as silliness can easily contage into more serious problems. This can happen so quickly that the adult never has a chance to regain control of the group. For example, a teacher was correcting a boy for making an inappropriate comment about a girl. Other students started laughing and making even more inappropriate comments. She finally told one of the students to leave and go to the office. But as that student was exiting, another taunted him saying, "Look, you got in trouble and I didn't. Ha ha." Now begins a new type of contagion as a conflict cycle escalates between those two boys.

Another dynamic is a pair of youth who have a mutually satisfying symbiotic relationship. For instance, George, the bully, and Vinny, his willing victim: Vinny was always running to the teacher: "George is doing this. George is doing that to me." But George is absent today, so Vinny comes to the teacher and asks, "Where is George? When's he coming back? I'm glad he isn't here." Except that it is a vacuum for Vinny because his main school activity is to get punished and put down by George. So they have this reciprocal arrangement. They have a lovely time together. Not healthy but satisfying.

It got so bad, the teacher forbade verbal aggression. "You stop calling Vinny those names." Period. Absolutely. So George just mouths them with no sound. Of course, Vinny knows exactly what George is doing, so he runs up to the teacher with: "He said it again." George says, "I didn't say a word. Nobody heard, you couldn't hear me. Did you hear me, Teach?" So then the teacher tightens the rules: "You can't even make your lips move." No read my lips allowed. So now George only *looks* at the target. But Vinny squeals, "He's looking at me. He's still bothering me." The teacher responds, "Well, why did you look at him?" Vinny says, "Well, I gotta see what he's doing." The tortured and torturer have a little arrangement. Until the nature of that relationship is resolved, the teacher is not going to be able to do much business with those youngsters.

Teachers have not been given much help in dealing with group dynamics, leadership, and conflict. They need to be able to bring out these problems and discuss them with students. "George, why do you like to make fun of Vinny?" "Oh, he's such a sissy." "And how do you feel when you have hurt his feelings?" George, the bully, wants Vinny to suffer, and you wonder what is behind this meanness. Soon you learn that George is always beaten up by his big brother at home. But here in school he has power, and it's just too juicy to resist. That's why we emphasize the life space interview to deal with a problem event, trace it to its roots, and explore alternative ways of handling the issue that lies behind the symptom. The same forces that work against us can be turned around.

Abdicating Responsibility

In a group situation, something goes wrong but no individual feels personal responsibility. We called this the "pie" phenomenon because everybody has a piece of the action, but all believe they are innocent. Each contributes to contagion and chaos but all say, "We didn't do nothing." For instance, a group of campers broke into some mailboxes and stole checks, all while hiking along the highway with their counselors. How did this happen on an innocent outing with adult supervision? It was fascinating to piece together what turned out to be a federal offense.

Children have group lives which are not shared with adults. Grownups think they are in charge, but a youth subculture operates at the same time. This particular group of campers was hiking along the highway with a little clique of delinquents lagging behind. The episode begins as one kid says, "Oh SEE the mailboxes." That was his little piece of the pie. Later, when we discuss the theft of checks, he claimed total innocence. "What about free speech? Can't you even say 'see the mailboxes'?"

If it weren't for the way he had said it, the second kid wouldn't have even noticed the mailboxes. But now, Boy #2 takes his piece of the pie and accepts the implied invitation to open and peek in the mailboxes.

Of course, he later disavowed any responsibility. "I just looked. I wouldn't take nothing out of them mailboxes. That's a B & E" (breaking and entering). By implication, he only did a B but not an E. Instead, he opens each mailbox and announces, "There's nothing in number one, some letters in number two," and so forth along this string of mailboxes.

Now Boy #3 comes along. Of course, he wouldn't have had anything to do with breaking in. "I wouldn't have. I wouldn't break in." However, once the boxes were open, he could enter guilt free. "After all, I didn't open the mailboxes." What he did was take out the envelopes and open them only to discover they contained checks. He doesn't want to get in trouble so he gives the checks to yet another boy, who distributes them among the group. Now there are many more pieces of the pie. Later the recipients of the checks would say to me, "Geez. A guy gives you some money, you shouldn't take it? Are you crazy?" It seems very reasonable to them that they didn't steal. They had nothing to do with anything bad. They just walked down a dusty road, but now they all had checks.

Then, one kid looks at his check. "Oh oh, this is over ten bucks." It seems he had a notion that stealing over ten dollars would get you in the big house. Under ten dollars, they just talk to you and nothing happens. So he takes his check and tears it up in front of the rest of them and drops the pieces. All of this is going on sub rosa in ways so adults don't know what is happening. As the torn pieces flutter down, the boy whispers to peers to explain his action. Now comes a new contagion as all the other boys decide to tear up their checks and throw them away.

Nobody has taken checks so nobody has anything to worry about. Except that the mailman has learned that something has happened and calls the Chicago office who send the State Police out to Fresh Air Camp. I called the entire group together and we are sitting there with the State Police, guns and all. I am supposed to be running the camp, but the police don't pay any attention to me, because this is way beyond me. It is not a camp thing. Of course, since none of the boys had "done anything," they just sit quietly and politely.

The police just want to get these boys to confess. Then it would be all right. It is the "say you are sorry" solution. But what the kids wanted to know from the cops was "How many guys did you shoot with that gun?"

The cops were trying to get them to be sorry and contrite and apologize and say they would not do it again. Nobody was talking so the cops decided to let the kids talk it over. "We are going outside and will be back in ten minutes and see what you have thought about this," they announce with a tone of authority, bolstered by their regalia of guns and bullet belts. It was really very funny except it was tragic.

When the cops returned, most of the kids caught on and were really sorry. "Geez. We shouldn't have done that. That was a very bad thing," as one boy recites his ritual of remorse. "It was bad because the lady's juice would be cut off if the electric bill wasn't paid." He explains why it was wrong and how he didn't think of all those things then but does now. He would never, ever do anything like that again, honest. The cop is very pleased with his recitation.

A couple of others catch on and make similar confessions. But one kid insists that he didn't do anything and kept demanding, "I want to call my court worker." That brought complications because none of the others wanted their court workers to show up. How can they make this boy confess like the rest of them? So the leader of the peer group gets down on his knees and begs for the holdout to "tell them you are sorry." But the boy still says, "I didn't do nothing. Why should I tell them I'm sorry?" The begging boy says, "Never mind. Just tell him you are sorry and we can all go swimming." It worked. Now everyone in the group had confessed and police would let them go. But not before giving one more warning. The boys were happy and wanted to know more about the guns and if the police had ever had a car chase.

Positive Group Cultures

The challenge of working with groups is to turn negative dynamics into positive group cultures.[58] In many group situations there seems almost no way to prevent the instant formation of negative cliques or wild stimulation. While individual work with particular members might get to the heart of their problems, the most powerful interventions serve to change the group dynamics.

One must spend considerable effort to induce positive elements in the peer culture. The tone of group life can be improved by group activities and fun trips, and camping has been specifically pertinent. Celebrations of birthdays or other positive events can build a group bond. Cooperative academic or extracurricular activities, such as producing a play, can foster a positive group. Much of the group tone will depend on how youth come to identify with and feel about the adult leader.

Initially, peer groups may look like a battleground where both adult and youth see one another as enemies. The core of changing this dynamic is trust. Among the most powerful interventions are to use group life space interviews, which is not a simple task. Again, contagion is in play and what starts as a sensible discussion can end in interpersonal flack. But the group is the largest reinforcing factor, and turning this in a positive direction is an important goal. Obviously groups have the potential for positive as well as negative outcomes, and this is an important ongoing area of study. There is great potential for using group discussions in the classroom and other settings in order to build cultures of care and concern.

A very young Bill Morse leaning against the window of the new house which he and Sunny built with their own hands as part of a five-family community in Ann Arbor in the late 1930s.

Bill and Sunny Morse at the time of their marriage.

The Morses with their children Susan and Jim at Fresh Air Camp.

Goin' Fishin' – and a little nervous.

Strolling back to the cabin.

Two troubled and angry campers.

A group life space interview. From left, Larry Brendtro, two campers, a counselor, Dave Wineman, and camp director Elton B. McNeil.

Some Close Colleagues of William Morse

Dr. Urie Bronfenbrenner (1917-2005) of Cornell University pioneered the ecological model that challenged deficit approaches to child psychology.

Cornell University Photography

Professor David Wineman (1916-1995) of Wayne State University School of Social Work was clinical director of Fresh Air Camp from 1950-1968 and co-authored *The Aggressive Child* with Fritz Redl.

Dr. Nicholas Long established the Life Space Crisis Intervention Institute. He and Bill Morse were co-authors of six editions of *Conflict in the Classroom*.

Dr. Ralph D. Rabinovitch founded Hawthorn Center, a model child and adolescent treatment program. Fritz Redl and Bill Morse were consultants.

Bill Morse at his "first retirement" from the University of Michigan in 1983.

Bill Morse and former student Larry Brendtro in 2006.

CHAPTER SEVEN

Assessment in the Life Space

What we need in order to work effectively with a child is not the category, especially those fantasy splits in DSM ... but a comprehensive understanding of each individual child.[59]

At Fresh Air Camp, we used to read the voluminous records on the children coming to camp to prepare us for a brief interview on their arrival. Sometimes record monsters turned out to be scared waifs, and "really nice little fellows" were skillful delinquents who began casing the camp as soon as they were off the bus. Records cannot tell us who the child might be. Only the human encounter of talking together can.

Diagnostic Rituals

Traditional assessment chops kids up in pieces so each profession can have its piece of the diagnostic pie. Essentially we have a bureaucratic system where all tasks are broken down to specifics. One discipline can only do this, another discipline can do that. Afterwards you take all these people who have seen their narrow piece of this kid and have a conference to put the puzzle together. I am not sure you would ever recognize the kid after the specialists assemble the pieces.

Different professions use a variety of diagnostic schemes that do not jibe. Psychiatry keeps publishing new editions of DSM, adding all kinds of supposed disorders. Psychologists have a host of assessment protocols and education is not far behind. Every discipline also defends its sacred rituals. Many social workers thought they were the only ones who really should seriously study families. Psychologists dominated diagnosis. As special educators gained new diagnostic tools, this competed with school psychology. Few remembered that there was a time when psychologists were not tied down with testing but consulted with teachers about how to make classrooms and school climates more hygienic for child growth.

When special education became syndicated, psychologists became the "deciders" by assessing who fit what category for service. In fact, studies showed that the school psychologist's data had undue influence in the meetings. Pronouncing "On the basis of these tests ..." carried a lot of clout. While test scores appear to be objective, they give a very incomplete understanding of the child. Most other team members did not know enough about what those numbers meant to challenge them. One teacher told me, "I don't understand much of it so it must be something important, Bill. It's beyond me." Ignorance bestowed great power, the "magic" of assessment.

I have written considerably on inter-professional collegiality in programs for disturbed children. Studies show there is very little linkage between diagnosis, Individual Education Plans, programs offered, and outcome. I think that is because assessment is concentrated on collecting flawed information which does not tell us where to direct our efforts.

As special education expanded, it developed bureaucratic "diseases" which required counter measures. One problem was that when we put challenging students in special education, they were likely to stay there. We forgot about them and didn't look at developmental growth and ecological changes. So the "re-eval" was invented to protect kids from being sidetracked in special education.

That cure caused a new disease as re-evaluation became a terrible time absorber. Schools were so busy testing kids and re-testing, they did not have time to digest the data that was collected. I used to meet regularly with psychologists to consult on challenging cases. But there was little time for reflection as they were rushing to get their tests done by the deadline.

The next countermeasure aimed to short-circuit evaluations because of overwhelming time expended. Consultation took the place of evaluation. But traditional consultation often ended up with teachers having more responsibilities and problems than before. They are told,

"You should do this and you should do that," but actually these "shoulds" are not feasible in the classroom setting.

A different style of working together was needed. Lynne Cook[60] and others developed cooperative or collaborative consultation. The process is quite different as participants join in problem-solving rather than performing a ritual professional dance. We look at the individual youngster and try to solve the problem, given this class and the group ecology of schools and other influences contributing to the child's life space.

The Power of One

We need to move from narrow theories to the study of the individual child. Kids cannot be squeezed into shape to fit some theory. The core of special education is the Individual Education Plan (IEP).[61] What is this person like and what help is most appropriate? These are tenets of individual psychology which studies the various forces contributing the development of a person.[62] When a narrow theory is applied to the person, it inevitably distorts the reality. Instead, the theory should come out of the child. It is emergent rather than imposed. Otherwise, we make kids over into all these different formats to fit our theory.

Nobody really knows how to help these kids in the thousand situations they are up against every day, each minute making decisions about what is right for the child and the group. Should you kick the kid out? Or try to calm him? What should you say? Constant decisions. I don't know how much value there is to "expertise in a vacuum."

We learn most by talking with a kid or spending time observing in a classroom or group setting. If the child doesn't know you, how are you going to learn much by conversing? But I find that children often enjoy explaining themselves. What I do is sit down with a child (often several together) and talk about a situation. One can begin by having them tell about highlights of their day. Social ecologists wrote an entire book on that: *One Boy's Day.*[63] You hopped on the bus; who else was on that bus? There was a fight on the bus? By the time they get to school, they are already stirred up for the day. Find out how they felt about what happened. You can learn a lot through brief life space interviews.

Kids have a lot to teach us. Once, I had a panel of students talk to professionals about what it was like to be emotionally impaired. They moved the audience in a way I could never do. I didn't censor them, so once a group of adolescents gets going, it's hard to tell what direction they might take. What I didn't know at the time was that the mother of one of the students had joined the professional meeting. When her son spoke, he talked of thoughts of suicide and family matters. After the meeting, she came up and said, "I'm the mother of so and so who was on your panel." I went into a state of panic. But we sat down and talked, and finally the boy came up to join the conversation. "You know," the mother said, "I never knew those things." Her son never talked to her about some of the things that were really on his mind. It turned out to be a positive experience because the mother was very insightful and caring.

As a psychologist, I was never trained how to write an honest report that a parent is going to see. In the old days, we hid reports so nobody saw them. Now it is an open book. The goal should be to always act in a way that anything said would not be hurtful to anybody. When I write a report about the child, I should be writing it to the student and his family as much as to the teacher or anybody else. We have to learn how to say hard things in ways that are as helpful as possible. With emotionally disturbed children, that's particularly difficult – we don't call a spade a spade because we're afraid we'll hurt somebody. In the deflection, we cause more damage. The child deserves to know about the problems without feeling worse because of that information.

Individual psychology matches special education principles by calling for individual interventions. What frequently happens is quite different. The pupil is a member of a classroom group which is taught as a unit rather than as individual learners. Many teachers believe it is not fair to treat students differently. That is a primitive, legalistic designation of fairness – everyone gets the same treatment, no matter if it helps or not. This contrasts with psychological fairness which is to provide each of us what that person needs.

We can help kids understand that not everybody needs the same treatment. If a student says, "You let so and so do it, you didn't let me do it," my answer was, "What are we trying to do for you? Is there a better way we can help you?" Each deserves the best that we can deliver and to treat all the same violates individual needs.

Individual psychology uses research techniques not very prevalent in the literature. Most research studies come out with generalized conclusions based upon a theoretical average. There may be no such kid. But we tell a teacher: This is what to expect if you teach the disturbed. They will be more this way or that than regular kids.

I read a lot of the journals and abstracts and try to keep up with the field. But it seems to me that most of the research is faulty in the sense it gives us notions that are not very accurate for the practitioner. So we started developing some other ideas about research.

Instead of studying group averages, we can use what is called the "N of 1" technology, which means research based on single subjects. There are two types of N of 1 research. Behaviorists study an isolated behavior in one kid and chart the performance, and then impose some change and chart subsequent behavior. That's one kind of N of 1, and I'm not talking about that, although it has its uses. I'm talking about an N of 1 in which you try to describe as many of the relevant aspects of the *child* and the *environment* as you can, and make predictions on the basis of that information.

The Ecological Perspective

Traditional diagnosis has focused too narrowly on the child's problems while ignoring the broader ecological system. We seldom spend as much time analyzing the forces which create problem behavior as we do talking about the kid's superficial symptoms. Instead, we need an ecological diagnosis which studies the child in his or her life space, responding to all kinds of external vectors of influence.[64]

Certain environments bring out certain behaviors so it is just as fruitful to study these ecologies as to probe the child. Our treatment or learning environments have different effects on different youth. For example, behavior modification can be a blessing or it can backfire. When you ask kids about it, some say, "It helps me know exactly what I should do." But many other children see point and level systems as adults hiding behind rules instead of helping them with problems. One teacher told me she had some 300 rules and punishments all listed in a folder that was as thick as a book. I asked her how they could have a rule for everything that could happen. She said, "Well, when something happens that we haven't got a rule for, we add a new rule." That kind of attitude infuriates many children. But almost any humane ecology can "work" if it fits the child's needs.

At Hawthorn Center, which serves very disturbed children, the school is a very supportive environment. Most of the time, kids are working independently or are receiving individual help. Teachers design the ecology to motivate and provide success. The curriculum is adapted to fit the child rather than making the child fit the curriculum. Teachers try to insure that the environment does not exacerbate the problems of the child. They unleash normal growth processes for therapeutic change.

When an environment is positive, negative behavior is minimized. For example, some students at Hawthorn Center thrive in the shop or the greenhouse where they learn through concrete experiences. Others learn the basics of food preparation or how to operate a restaurant. Academics are integrated with lots of arithmetic, language, and social learning. When educational ecology is relevant and meets needs, positive behavior ensues.

When we were in the camp, psychologists could not give a battery of tests to a kid until they had followed him around for a day. By that time, frequently they did not need to give the tests. In schools what we ask is that a psychologist not give a test until he has seen the kid's portfolio, (which might be a mess), his desk with the pictures he's drawn and the stuff he's done, and has had some assessment of the child's behavior performance. These data and observations are often more potent than artificial sampling of behavior on an achievement or personality test. We should be required first to collect information on the child's functioning in his or her various ecologies. It isn't that you don't use formal diagnostic materials, but you use them selectively.

Ralph Rabinovitch told me that he never interviews a youngster before he knows what the problem is. He gets this from the records, developmental knowledge, and biological factors. But he doesn't know what shape the problem will take with the specific child. His point is: "If a kid has been maligned like this and I have a good case and family history, I will know somehow what is hurting that youngster. But I'll never know how the child formulates all of this until I talk to the individual child."

As we understand the child in his life space, we can get beyond trying to use all of these tests and scales. We place a great deal of emphasis on the initial interview with a student. This is where the social bond is established. We use a time line where the child traces significant events in his or her life (with the help of record data). Suppose the student has lived in 12 different home settings. What might these "rejections" have meant to the child?[65] Any kid who has been repeatedly uprooted is going to have a problem with feeling that anybody cares about him no matter how loving somebody tries to be momentarily.

We can do a *lifeline* to identify significant life events that have shaped this youngster's behavior, values, and thinking. We try to understand the life story of a youngster and identify significant persons in their world. We have them talk about who they have contact with during the day. They teach us about supportive and stressful people and events in their current environment. What are important memories of school? Who did the child live with and what was going on at different points in life? We also have the youngster project the future. "What do you want to be when you're grown up?"

I found the lifeline helps teachers understand difficult students. They begin to shake their heads: "He is only eight years old and he has lived in that many different homes?" They begin to feel for that child, to empathize. That's why the literature section in *Conflict in the Classroom*[66] is so important, because, through the stories, the reader feels what the world is like as seen by the child.

While we want to approach the child respectfully, we must remember that any assessment processes can be unnerving to youngsters. Interviews, tests, and observations have an invasive quality. Children don't know why they are being scrutinized, and afterward they aren't sure what they might have revealed. If I'm giving tests, I should prepare them for what we will do and afterwards share some results. "Now this is what we've done." I will have some idea in general of what that kid's strengths or weaknesses might be and should be honest with him, but so gentle because it's a very threatening condition.

Nobody wants to have oneself arbitrarily revealed to others in the ways we force on children. Rabinovitch taught me that you never open up a child without closing the youngster up again before leaving their presence. You don't want this kid who has told you all of these things to leave with emotions stirred up, feeling it was a mistake to tell you the terrible things that have happened to him. I don't think that is a humane way to treat people who have exposed part of their inner life.

When a child reveals a problem to an adult, he expects us to do something about it, to be of help. We give them some reason to believe that there is some way out of this problem and that somebody will be at their side. We talk with children about hope and we have to follow-through, because a child should not be left naked in the snowstorm after we're done with the session. We leave children with hope.

CHAPTER EIGHT

Hope Regenerates

When we realize that it is our own salvation that is involved,
I suspect we will embrace new concepts more vigorously.[67]

To advocate for children has been a career-long battle. I think I resented formal retirement at the time, but I was very fortunate to continue my involvement with universities and consulting with educational programs. But you get old, and I'm not so sure that you don't ossify. Some pioneers seem by nature to be as creative and as at home with the conflicts and problems of youth today as they were in the time when they cut their eye teeth on serving special kids. But these people have to be very careful about "arrogant age wisdom." Parents often say to a child, "When you're as old as I am…." They're not as old as you so the adult always has an ace in the hole. Only it backfires because kids don't believe it. They say, "You don't know what life is like now."

People who have been recognized as experts have to be careful for the same reason. It's very flattering for me to be telling this history, but you have to be careful not to think that just because you've lived longer, you are wiser. We have to be careful that people with stature and influence don't convey arrogance and old solutions to new problems. They have to keep involved in the work. In my field, kids are more maligned. Terrible case histories. Multiple disabilities. More tragic families. More depression. I cannot work from the base of my past experience alone. I have to do the same as I always had to do: see what the real problems are and work in a collaborative way with people who are on the firing line. Maybe then I can say, "Look, we once had that crisis teacher, and that seemed to help. So why don't you resurrect that notion and bring needed support to kids today?"

History is valuable as older people may know some things that once were important and are still appropriate today. But they should not pontificate on the past. With that caution, I conclude by sharing what seem to be enduring principles to guide our work in any time or place.[68]

Growth goals apply to all children and adolescents. The first element in a psychologically healthy environment is interaction within the family which respects and protects children. We are also concerned with their involvement and commitment to school and participation in the broader world. We want to maximize their intelligence, ability to relate to others, sense of self worth, inner directedness, and hopes for the future.

Deep values permeate the life space. These determine how our children relate to others and how they will grow and develop. We do not design our schools or youth programs around "rules for adult comfort." Rather, the milieu code is responsive to young people and values their participation. In time of crisis, problem-solving is non-punitive and provides support for both youth and their caregivers. For deep change to occur, the total life space must reflect values of concern for others.

Caring adults model the same goals and values that we hold for children. Adults are neither authoritarian nor do they join with the youth peer culture. Instead, they embrace democratic ways of relating to children in our ongoing life experiences with them. This does not suggest that parents or teachers are perfect but that they make a conscious effort to display in concrete behavior that which we want our children to become.

Authentic education blends both cognitive and affective goals. A rich array of curriculum is available to use literature and the arts to allow children to express themselves and understand others. Art, play, music, dance, and drama are natural ways for children to externalize and deal with feelings. However, these affective activities must not be over-emphasized as is now the case with cognitive learning. Instead, they are incorporated into the life stream of education.

Peer relationships are often the youngster's most potent teacher. Any educational or treatment design which does not enlist the power of the peer culture leaves real influence to chance. Many of our children are group addicts who get all of their life meaning from interaction with peers. Adults need to reassert influence, but not through force and repression. Instead, we can use the group process to teach new codes of values and ways of interacting with others.

Therapeutic resources are needed for families and children who are distraught and in crisis. Too often we seek to deal with disturbed children as if they have no problems when they need help in decoding their troubled lives. We must direct our efforts at building the competence of those who spend the most time in the life space of our children. We must help them develop the knowledge and commitment necessary to maximize the potentials of all of our youngsters.

I am often asked by my students, "What keeps you going?" Well, on odd days of the week I get depressed, not just about our field but the state of the country. Then on even days, hope regenerates, especially when I visit teachers who are doing great things for children.[69]

Roots and Wings: Pioneers and Their Legacy
Larry K. Brendtro

If I have seen further, it is by standing on the shoulders of giants.[1]
Sir Isaac Newton

A Pioneer in Our Times

William Morse often spoke of the need to attend to both depth and spread to understand troubled children. His own career could be aptly described with those terms. His experience across nearly seven decades tapped into the great pioneers of the past century and left his own legacy that endures in an army of students and colleagues.

All who knew Bill remark about his ability to blend rigorous scientific thought with a profound commitment to society's most troubled and troubling young persons. Tom McIntyre, Hunter College of City University of New York, observes:

> Dr. Morse talks affectionately and humorously about kids who others speak of with disdain. He teaches us to decode the inter-personal calls for help that are frequently disguised in messages of disruption, rancor, and confrontation. We are then directed to reach through the barbed wire defenses that entangle or repel so many professionals who wish to help wayward young people, but don't know yet how to do so. In educational and mental health domains dominated by diagnostic categories, standardized assessment, and rigid practice models, he provides a clear unobstructed view of how misguided minds and behaviors are redirected through development of trusting relationships.

In this final section, we put Morse's philosophy and career in perspective, showing his links with early pioneers in reclaiming children and youth and his seminal role in the reclaiming youth revolution.

The Roots of Reclaiming Philosophies

At the dawn of the 1900s, fresh approaches to education and youth work flourished. Swedish sociologist Ellen Key (1909) heralded this era as *The Century of the Child* where democratic values and modern science would replace autocratic approaches. Maria Montessori (1948) implemented these ideas in schools designed to tap the *absorbent minds* of children from the slums of Rome. August Aichhorn (1925) of Austria demonstrated the power of building therapeutic relationships with *wayward youth*. Alfred Adler (1930) developed new approaches to *the problem child* based on a deep understanding of the young person's *private logic* and goals. Janusz Korczak (1967) enlisted street kids from the Warsaw Ghetto as *citizens in embryo* in self-governing residential schools. Kurt Lewin (1948) conducted *action research* on society's most challenging problems, contending that science was not neutral but a potential force for positive change. Finally, youth themselves were central in this transformation. Gisela Konopka described the Wandervogel youth movement where adults teamed with idealistic youth in the struggle to transform schools and youth programs to reflect democratic ideals (Andrews, 2000).

This period of great optimism was to be cut short. As the clouds of war gathered over Europe, dreams of a Century of the Child were deferred. The positive group spirit of the Wandervogel era was replaced with the Hitler Youth Movement. Many progressive educators were executed and their books were burned. But scores of world-renowned pioneers in psychology, education, and youth work escaped Hitler's onslaught by moving to North America. Through this random event of history, many European intellectuals were "Exiled into Paradise" (Heilbut, 1983). Now even more deeply committed to democratic principles, they replanted the seeds of change in more fertile soil.

Two of the most influential of these pioneers were practice theorist Kurt Lewin (1890-1947) and theory practitioner Fritz Redl (1902-1988).

Lewin coined the term "life space" to emphasize that individual behavior must be understood in its social ecology. Redl applied those principles in the *life space interview*, which moved therapy to the frontline of work with troubled children. Redl would spend a long career working at Wayne State University in Detroit. Lewin would die in the prime of his life, and his colleagues would carry forth his research at the University of Michigan.

In a twist of geopolitical history, Michigan became the rallying point for the reclaiming youth movement. Its network of progressive universities, schools, and youth programs provided practical laboratories for action research in new methods. Protégés of Lewin and Redl would make seminal contributions to education and the behavioral sciences.[2]

Bullock and Menendez (1999) put Michigan at the roots of the movement to serve children with emotional and behavioral disorders. Fritz Redl created programs for aggressive inner city youth, Ralph Rabinovitch developed one of the nation's finest facilities for treatment of children with emotional problems, William Cruickshank transformed Michigan's training school for delinquents, and various Michigan universities began training teachers for troubled students. This epilogue highlights how pioneers inspired with a reclaiming ethos have transformed currrent approaches to challenging children and adolescents.

Kurt Lewin   *Fritz Redl*

Restorative Relationships

Successful educational and treatment environments build positive relationships and use problems as opportunities for learning and growth. Just such a setting was described in August Aichhorn's classic 1925 book *Wayward Youth*. He and Anna Freud trained a young psychologist, Fritz Redl, who brought these ideas to the United States. Redl soon gained prominence as a noted authority on work with troubled children and youth.

Redl was instrumental in developing therapeutic camping programs which also served as hands-on training laboratories for aspiring professionals. He taught first at the University of Michigan and then at Wayne State University. There he and social work professor David Wineman completed their exhaustive 1957 study, *The Aggressive Child*, which is considered a landmark in qualitative research (Smith, 2004).

Redl and Wineman enlisted their graduate students to live 24/7 with highly aggressive boys in a group setting called Pioneer House. Using Lewin's action research principles, they documented in minute detail exactly how these boys behaved in their natural life space, showing both their problems and also their considerable strength and resilience. They developed specific practical methods to manage "surface behavior" as well as in-depth interventions designed to build positive relationships and values. They used "life space interviews" with children in times of conflict to help them develop "controls from within."

Redl and Wineman teamed with William C. Morse at the University of Michigan Fresh Air Camp where a generation of graduate students learned these reclaiming strategies. After directing the camp for 15 years, Morse was succeeded by Elton B. McNeil, professor of psychology at the university. McNeil observed that "The camp has done more than keep pace with the Psychological Age, it has helped to pioneer it and has contributed significantly to the growth of the behavioral sciences" (McNeil, 1962, p. 118).

Morse is arguably the 20th century's preeminent leader in the education of troubled students. He began his career in the 1940s and remained professionally active for 60 years. Morse published a dozen books and monographs, including a national study of public school programs for emotionally handicapped students commissioned by the

Council for Exceptional Children (Morse, Cutler, & Fink, 1964). That research showed that school staff often used green thumb, primitive, or chaotic approaches.

To address the lack of training of teachers, Morse and his former student Nicholas Long published the first edition of the authoritative text, *Conflict in the Classroom*. This psychoeducational text is unparalleled in its six editions running from 1965 through the current volume published in 2007 by Long, Morse, Fecser, and Newman. Described in a recent review, "This book evidences a humanistic philosophy that embraces the worth of each young person and teaching methods that feature relationship building and valuation of children" (Ackerman & Hoover, 2008, p. 34).

Morse and Redl also collaborated with child psychiatrists Ralph D. Rabinovitch and his wife, Sara Dubo, who directed Hawthorn Center, a widely acclaimed child and adolescent treatment center. The four of them founded what was perhaps the first statewide organization to empower families as advocates for their emotionally disturbed children. Rabinovitch explained:

> This was an extension of earlier experience conducting group therapy with parents of troubled children. We learned how lonely and isolated so many of those parents felt. When they got together, they realized they weren't the only ones. There was a tremendous strength in their unity and relationship.[3]

More than a half century later, that organization still advocates on behalf of families for appropriate treatment of troubled youth excluded from schools or discarded in the correctional system.

The Ecology of Children

Morse always referred to troubled students as having ***socio***emotional problems to shift the focus from deficits in the child to relationships in the life space. This reflects Kurt Lewin's belief that studying the *social ecology* of natural relationships yields more useful information than isolated experiments. For example, the book *One Boy's Day* is a classic ecological account of one day in the life of a boy named Raymond. It is the most exhaustive account ever created on the influence of family, school, peers, and community on the behavior of a child (Barker & Wright, 1951). Lewin believed that natural observations and interactions were the best way to understand children.

Lewin's theories were put into practice by Urie Bronfenbrenner. They first met during World War II when Urie entered the military, fresh with a PhD from the University of Michigan. He was assigned to Lewin, who then worked for the Office of Special Services. Their team of psychologists was charged with selecting undercover agents. The aspiring spies were not given the typical psychological tests. Instead, they had to assume their new identities while living in a group at a secret location on a farm near Washington, DC. Every detail of their behavior was studied to see how they might act behind enemy lines.

A long professional lifespan gives opportunity for one's ideas to take root. Urie Bronfenbrenner (2005) spent the next six decades at Cornell University where he established the *bio-ecological model* of human development. Before Bronfenbrenner, specialties like psychology, neuroscience, sociology, and anthropology operated in isolation. He built bridges between these disciplines to paint a clearer picture of the process of positive child and youth development.

Bronfenbrenner's most basic belief was that trusting bonds with children are the most powerful force in building healthy brains and behavior. He translated this principle into simple but powerful terms: *Every child needs at least one adult who is irrationally crazy about him or her.* Young people thrive in ecologies with caring families, concerned teachers, positive peers, and a supportive community.

The ecological model challenged the very notion of "disturbance" or "disorder" as a flaw in the child. Instead of diagnosing "disease" in the child, the focus was on "dis-ease" in the ecology. Interventions sought to strengthen family and school bonds and foster positive peer and community influence.

Nicholas Hobbs (1982), once president of the American Psychological Association, applied ecological principles to emotionally disturbed children in the Re-Education (Re-ED) model. He also drew concepts from the holistic European educateur profession to break free from polarized debates between psychodynamic and behavioral proponents. A copy of his book, *The Troubled and Troubling Child*, is autographed: "To Urie Bronfenbrenner, longtime colleague and cherished friend, with admiration and appreciation."[4]

The Re-ED model had solid research support and was on a track to become federal policy in juvenile justice and mental health, but the Vietnamese war dried up funding. However, Re-ED thrived in the non-profit sector.[5] Other ecological models branding themselves as *multi-system* or *family system* approaches are extensions of the pioneering work of Bronfenbrenner and Hobbs (Cantrell & Cantrell, 2007).

William Rhodes and Matt Trippe were part of the team who created Re-ED (Cruickshank, 1974). Subsequently, they joined the faculty of the University of Michigan. Rhodes (1972) authored a major study of competing theories of child *variance*, a less judgmental label for what others called *deviance*. Morse and Smith (1980) turned this into a video training course where episodes of problem behavior were analyzed by various theory experts.

Trippe became director of the Fresh Air Camp after Elton B. McNeil retired. However, he was less connected to the therapeutic tradition and shifted the camp to a special education focus. Clinical director David Wineman, the longest serving senior faculty, resigned in 1968. Had he not been diagnosed with multiple sclerosis, Trippe might have found the challenges of running the camp less daunting, but it closed during his tenure. Table 1 provides a brief historical chronology of the Fresh Air Camp.

In yet another random event, Matt Trippe extended the reclaiming philosophy to Starr Commonwealth, Michigan's leading school for troubled boys. He was hired by the Starr Board of Directors to help conduct a search for a successor to Floyd Starr, its 84-year-old founder. Trippe recruited his Fresh Air Camp colleague, Larry Brendtro, who would lead Starr Commonwealth for fourteen years. In a plan of succession, Brendtro's colleagues Arlin Ness and Martin Mitchell gave long-term continuity to the reclaiming philosophy in a high profile program. Starr became an exemplar of programs to build positive peer group cultures as envisioned by Redl, Wineman, and Morse.

A Brief Chronological History
University of Michigan Fresh Air Camp[1]

1921	Founded by Student Christian Association as outdoor experience for underprivileged youths.
1937	Graduate students begin working at camp
1941	Fritz Redl comes to camp: "milieu therapy" introduced
1944	University of Michigan accepts ownership of camp
1945	William C. Morse appointed Director
1950	David Wineman assumes clinical leadership responsibilities
1960	Morse resigns; Elton B. McNeil assumes administrative responsibilities.
1967	McNeil resigns; Matthew J. Trippe assumes administrative and fundraising responsibilities. Academic-focused programming introduced.
1968	Wineman resigns. Conclusion of "The Golden Years"[2]
1969-1979	Focus on special education teacher training.
1980	Camp closed as training laboratory; rented for private uses.

⌒

[1]Archives on the U. of M. Fresh Air Camp are found in the University of Michigan Bentley Library

[2]Annie Marshak Dowling, 2006. *A pictorial history of the University of Michigan Fresh Air Camp 1921-2005* in which she labels the 1950s-1960s as "The Golden Years."

The Gang Under the Couch

From the life space perspective, therapeutic relationships are not confined to the formal office-based counseling hour but permeate "the other 23 hours" (Trieschman, Whittaker, & Brendtro, 1969). But when adults try to build therapeutic relationships, the gang is under the couch, observed Redl (1966). He and Lewin wrote profusely about peer group dynamics.

Lewin and colleagues studied children's groups in camps, schools, and other natural settings. They compared permissive, authoritarian, and democratic climates. Groups with *laissez faire* adult leadership were marked by chaos and conflict. On the opposite pole, *authoritarian* leaders constantly barked out orders and sought to exercise control. However, *democratic* leaders provided more subtle influence and encouraged groups to develop responsibility and self-discipline. In recent years, some authors substitute the tougher sounding term *authoritative* in place of *democratic*, which confounds the core values behind Lewin's research.

Differences between authoritarian and democratic leadership were dramatic. Democratic groups were more cohesive and showed more respect to peers and adults in authority. Members worked cooperatively towards group goals and willingly helped one another. In contrast, youngsters in authoritarian groups were self-centered, seldom even using the pronoun "we" in their conversations. Many rebelled against authority or competed in trying to please the all-powerful adult. Lippitt and White explain:

> A vicious cycle of ego involvement developed in the aggressive reaction to authoritarian situations, for as competition for social approval from "the source" increased, the boys became less inclined to recognize with approval the work of one another. (1943, p. 505)

A wealth of studies show the positive effect of democratic processes, the ineffectiveness of permissive groups, and the negative effects of autocratic groups (White & Lippitt, 1960). Children who have punitive teachers show more aggression and are less concerned with school learning and values (Kounin & Gump, 1961). Such studies led to the creation of cooperative learning by associates of Lewin (Schmuck & Schmuck, 2001). But in our current climate of control, this classic research on democratic groups is often overlooked as a solution to changing youth subcultures in schools and other group settings.

Democratic Group Climates

John Dewey first pioneered philosophies of democracy in education while teaching at the University of Michigan (Williams, 1998). Gordon Allport (1948) saw a "striking kinship" between the ideas of Dewey and Kurt Lewin. Both believed that democracy must be learned anew in each generation, and it is a far more difficult social structure to attain and to maintain than autocracy.

The first major attempt to apply democratic peer group research to practice was a five-year experimental study of Guided Group Interaction. This was a residential setting for delinquent youth and operated at the Highfields mansion in New Jersey, formerly owned by aviator Charles Lindbergh. The program enlisted delinquents in helping one another solve their problems (McCorkle, Elias, & Bixby, 1958).

Sociologist Ashley Weeks (1958) compared Highfields residents with those from a typical youth reformatory. Twelve months after release, the Highfields approach was decisively more effective. David Wineman (1960) reviewed that study and concluded that the samples, while not random, were comparable and improvements were genuine. He called for more research on the nature of changes occurring in the personalities of the youth:

> We desperately need prolific experimentation in residential treatment of youth with serious behavior problems so let us salute Highfields as a courageous and hopefully permanent step in this direction. (1960, p. 120)

The Highfields research was also analyzed by psychiatrist Richard Jenkins (1958). His earlier studies at the University of Michigan found two distinct pathways to delinquency (Hewitt & Jenkins, 1946). Socialized delinquents came from neighborhoods with poverty and high crime rates but basically had intact interpersonal skills. Unsocialized delinquents had experienced much disruption of early relationships and were highly frustrated and emotionally troubled. Gold and Osgood (1992) would later label these youth as *buoyant* and *beset*. Although the buoyant group adapted best to groups, Jenkins (1958) saw positive potential effects with both types of youth:

> Guided Group Interaction at Highfields encourages the re-examination of such psychological defenses of the delinquent as stereotyped, negative, and hostile attitudes toward authority, toward others, and toward the community. The group no longer automatically backs up the hostile rationalizations of the delinquent but rather provides an atmosphere for their re-examination and modification. The group discussions also favor recognition of frustration reactions for what they are – maladaptive responses. The group influence, to

this extent, becomes a positive factor rather than the negative one it usually is. (pp. 152-153)

Harry Vorrath, who had received social work training at Highfields, established a national training center for Positive Peer Culture (PPC). This model was adopted in the 1970s by Michigan's major public and private programs for delinquent youth. Vorrath was invited to move to Starr Commonwealth where he and Starr's president Larry Brendtro co-authored the first treatment manual on *Positive Peer Culture* (Vorrath & Brendtro, 1974/1985).[6] William Morse described PPC as a "godsend" since methods to form positive peer groups were the missing link in this field:

> We have needed a group process which is relevant to professional and lay workers alike. It must be explicit so that all can understand. It must involve the youth themselves. (Morse, 1974, dust jacket copy)

PPC is a peer-helping model designed to cultivate strengths in troubled and troubling youth. "Care and concern" for others is the defining element of PPC. Rather than demanding obedience to authority or peers, PPC demands responsibility. Caring is made fashionable and any hurting behavior is totally unacceptable. As group members learn to trust, respect, and take responsibility for the actions of self and others, pro-social values, beliefs, and behaviors are established (Opp & Unger, 2006).

It is one thing to form groups and quite another to make deep changes in children or organizations. Many programs did not commit to the principle of teaching values instead of rules and tried to maintain parallel authoritarian structures. In such settings, peer group influence became just another club for superficial compliance. Gisela Konopka was one of the first to note the uneven fidelity between the ideals of PPC and its reality in practice. Her observations stimulated careful ongoing studies of what is required to train staff and change organizational cultures in order to make deep lasting changes in youth (Brendtro & Ness, 1985; Wasmund & Tate, 2000; Brendtro, Mitchell, & McCall, in press).

John Gibbs, Bud Potter, and Arnold Goldstein (1995) worked to insure the fidelity of PPC by enabling youth to become more skillful peer helpers. Their EQUIP program provides youth with additional training in social skills, emotional management, and pro-social thinking.

Outcome research using this adaptation of PPC has been very favorable and most well-established PPC programs now incorporate many of these strategies.

For a century, there has been concern that putting together groups of "deviant" youth would produce negative peer subcultures; the Positive Peer Culture model is specifically designed to counter this group contagion (Osgood, 2006). The most exhaustive studies of peer group treatment with delinquents is that of Gold and Osgood (1992). They studied youth in PPC programs at Starr Commonwealth, Boysville, and two Michigan state training schools. In contrast to the negative subculture that typifies such settings, they found that peer helping programs created a climate of safety. Their study suggests that attachment to adults and peers, achievement in school, a sense of autonomy, and peer helping can create an environment where treatment and growth is possible.

Reclaiming Strategies

New philosophies sprang from the democratic ideals of pioneering educators and youth workers in many cultures. The actual term "reclaiming" was first applied to troubled youth by Yochanan Wozner (1982) of Israel, who expanded Redl's concept of the therapeutic milieu. Wozner found that effective reclaiming environments have a "unifying theme." All stakeholders share a common mission of meeting the needs of young people.

What do all children need to grow and thrive? Larry Brendtro, Martin Brokenleg, and Steve Van Bockern (1990, 2002) wrote *Reclaiming Youth at Risk,* outlining the Circle of Courage resilience model. This taps the vision of reclaiming pioneers, the wisdom of tribal cultures, and modern resilience research (Brendtro & Larson, 2006; Seita & Brendtro, 2005). Following Circle of Courage principles, all young persons need opportunities to meet the need for Belonging, Mastery, Independence, and Generosity. These principles have been applied to a wide range of educational and treatment settings (Villa & Thousand, 2000; Lantieri, 2001). A common goal is to tap the strengths of troubled youth (Brendtro & Shahbazian, 2004; McCluskey & Mays, 2004).

Fritz Redl (1976) used *natural events* in the child's everyday experience as teaching and treatment opportunities. This concept was validated by research from Martin Hoffman (2000) of New York University who began studying empathy and moral development at the University of Michigan. Hoffman found that when discipline problems are used to help youngsters reflect on their behavior, self-control and conscience are strengthened. He calls this *inductive discipline* and it is contrasted with less effective methods of *power assertion or love withdrawal.*

Two reclaiming programs, RAP and LSCI, both harness the power of natural teaching moments. RAP is an acronym for Response Ability Pathways. This is a universal design training for all who are concerned with challenging youth. It was piloted by Larry Brendtro and Lesley du Toit (2005) in South Africa when Nelson Mandela, the first democratically elected president, called for a total transformation of services to young people at risk. His Minister of Welfare, Geraldine Fraser Moleketi, appointed Lesley du Toit to  manage this transformation. The Circle of Courage became the core philosophy behind youth policy, and RAP training was established to put this model into practice.

Response Ability Pathways is relevant to work with children and youth across cultures and settings. RAP strenghtens three natural abilities in both youth and their mentors: *Connect* for support, *Clarify* challenges, and *Restore* harmony. When all in an organization are trained in RAP, this provides the unifying belief system to meet needs of youth as proposed by Yochanan Wozner. A preliminary outcome study showed that teachers participating in RAP training were more cooperative in their orientation to students and were more likely to solve problems without resorting to restrictive interventions (Forthun & McCombie, 2007). The process of RAP is demonstrated in Figure 1.

Figure 1

Response **A**bility **P**athways

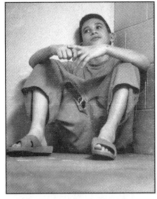

CONNECT
with persons in need.

CLARIFY
challenges and problems.

RESTORE
harmony and respect.

From Brendtro & du Toit, 2005. Photography is by Steve Liss (2005) from
No Place for Children: Voices from Juvenile Detention, University of Texas Press.

Life Space Crisis Intervention (LSCI) provides advanced therapeutic skills for persons who counsel youth in times of conflict (Long, Wood, & Fecser, 2001). Specific events are explored to identify the beliefs, feelings, and actions leading to self-defeating behavior. Reclaiming interventions address six types of problems: negative peer influence, limited social skills, weak conscience, distortion of reality, problems imported from home or street, and impulsivity with guilt. The table below shows how these LSCI interventions serve to meet Circle of Courage growth needs. Carol Dawson (2003) compared students in two junior high school programs for youth who are emotionally disturbed. Among significant outcomes in the LSCI school were reduction in the number of crisis incidents and a larger number of students who could return to mainstream schools. Staff also reported confidence in handling crisis situations.

How LSCI Reclaiming Interventions Meet Circle of Courage Growth Needs

1. **Imported problems:** This intervention is for youngsters who carry in problems from home or street and displace their distress on others. The goal is to manage problems and gain positive support. Developing self-control and support fosters mastery and belonging.

2. **Errors in perception:** These problems arise from distortions in thinking or perception that lead to maladaptive behavior. The goal is to help a youth think clearly and understand reality. Developing clear thinking fosters mastery and responsibility.

3. **Delinquent pride:** This involves students who are purposely aggressive and exploit others but do not feel appropriate guilt for their behavior. The goal is to help a youth feel empathy and concern for others. Developing empathy fosters generosity.

4. **Impulsivity and guilt:** This pattern involves youth who feel guilty about impulsive acts but lack confidence and self-worth. The goal is to strengthen inner controls on behavior. Developing self-control fosters independence.

5. **Limited social skills:** This involves youth who have appropriate motivation but lack the tools for success. The goal is to teach specific skills that enhance the youth's coping ability. Developing social skills can help the youth meet belonging, mastery, and other needs.

6. **Vulnerability to peer influence:** This intervention involves youth who let peers manipulate them into destructive behaviors. The goal is to manage self without being a pawn of peers. Developing inner control fosters independence.

From Brendtro & Long, 2005

Morse long advocated for ecological approaches to evaluation. He believed interviews with children were usually more useful than impersonal psychometric instruments (Morse, 1985). Traditional assessment is also deficit based, while reclaiming philosophies focus on strengths. In Redl's (1966) vernacular, this meant searching for the "virtues of delinquents."

A recent strength-based assessment model using reclaiming principles is *The Developmental Audit.*® Young persons participate in sharing their stories and developing a positive assessment and intervention plan (Brendtro, du Toit, Bath, & Van Bockern, 2007; Wood, et al., 1999). The Audit can be used in education, treatment, juvenile justice, and community settings. Like an accordion, it can be expanded or truncated to produce rapid assessments, ongoing education and treatment plans, or comprehensive risk assessments.

The Audit has three steps: 1) scan connections in the child's ecology, 2) identify patterns of resilient and self-defeating behavior and logic, and 3) develop a restorative plan. The Audit can also be adapted for use in a team meeting. The focus of discussion is to identify the function of behavior by examining **CLEAR** data: *Challenges, Logic, Emotions, Actions,* and *Results* (Koehler, 2006). The Audit is unique in that the young person is seen as the best expert on his or her life (Seita & Brendtro, 2005). The student and other key players in the life space provide necessary data for assessment and planning goals for growth.

From Yesterday to Tomorrow

The reclaiming pioneers searched for strengths in the most troubled youth. But many current approaches to education and treatment are inherently pessimistic, preoccupied with punishment or pathology. Our challenge is "to link yesterday with today and tomorrow"(Bullock & Gable, 1999). Now, a new strength-based revolution is underway. The American Psychological Association has called for a course correction towards a new positive psychology of prevention (Peterson & Seligman, 2004; Seligman & Csikszentmihalyi, 2000). As Erik Laursen (2008) proposes, this will require the purposeful design of cultures to create respectful alliances among youth and with elders. We need to keep children safe from harm but also attend to universal developmental needs of belonging, mastery, independence, and generosity.

The legacy of the reclaiming youth movement grew from the toil and wisdom of remarkable pioneers. While giants like Redl and Morse are gone, their spirit continues. The Council for Children with Behavior Disorders advocates for this population of needy youth. Reclaiming Youth International, the Life Space Crisis Intervention Institute, and Circle of Courage Institute are all training professionals worldwide. The journal *Reclaiming Children and Youth* is the mouthpiece for this movement, having published over 1000 leading-edge articles.[7] The internet is a new avenue for sharing ideas. The vibrant Child and Youth Care website posts a wealth of information including summaries of major journal articles in the reclaiming field.[8] The Psychoeducational Network website, which has now been dedicated to William Morse, offers analysis of all reclaiming programs.[9]

The University of Michigan Fresh Air Camp was once the laboratory for demonstrating reclaiming principles. Today that responsibility has been passed to a new generation of flagship organizations. Starr Commonwealth in Michigan and Ohio and Woodland Hills in Minnesota are models of democratic group cultures with delinquent youth. An international network of Re-ED programs and Circle of Courage schools is another modern legacy of the reclaiming movement. These are but a few representatives of the worldwide network of professionals and programs carrying forth the mission of reclaiming all of our children and youth.

Final Thoughts

It seems most fitting that Ralph Rabinovitch, now himself 92 years of age, be considered the leading expert on the lifelong contributions of his close friend and colleague, William C. Morse. At Bill's first attempted retirement in 1983, Dr. Rabinovitch noted that beneath Bill's prestigious formal vita is a deeper story.

"No one I know has touched more lives more positively than Bill Morse. He has been the incredibly available perceptor, advisor, and confessor to over two generations of students and colleagues. Bill has impacted the lives of countless disturbed children and their families, and this, I think, pleased him most."

Shortly after Bill Morse passed away, I had an opportunity to speak with Dr. Rabinovitch. He shared this final perspective about the many years they worked together in Michigan:

From the very beginning, we considered Hawthorn Center a school with a psychiatric program. Bill was the best antidote that I ever knew for burnout in teachers because he absorbed their problems. When he saw the tension, he was so benign, reassuring, and practical that it really helped tremendously. We had a lot of very difficult kids. If you ever want to talk about teaching through relationship, that would be Bill Morse because everyone loved him.

While interviewing Bill Morse in preparation for this publication, I remarked that whenever I tried to focus on his contributions, he would shine the light on others. So I said, "Bill, pretend this is your last lecture. You have a certain humility which makes it unfair for me to ask you this, but tell me, how you would like to be remembered?

Bill then shared this response: "Sometimes if I made a speech, there would be people who would say 'you must have been in my class.' I was seeing what they saw. Every once in a while, students from way back will contact me or I hear about them. They say that what we did in some of those awful university classes had meaning to them and that they are carrying on the ideas that we discussed. I would say that is the greatest satisfaction that I have. You never know what impact you have."

Bibliography

Ackerman, E., & Hoover, J. (2008). Conflict in the classroom: A review. *Reclaiming Children and Youth, 16*(4), 34-36.

Adler, A. (1930). *The problem child.* New York: G. P. Putnam's Sons.

Aichhorn, A. (1935). *Wayward youth.* New York: Viking Press. [Originally published in German in 1925.]

Allport, G. (1948). Foreword. In K. Lewin, *Resolving social conflicts.* Reprinted 2006. Washington, DC: American Psychological Association.

Anderson, I. H., & Dearborn, W. F. (1952). *The psychology of teaching reading.* New York: Ronald Press Company.

Andrews, J. (2000) Gisela Konopka and group work. *Encyclopedia of informal education,* www.infed.org/thinkers/konopka.htm

Bandura, A. (1986). *Social foundations of thought and action: A social cognitive theory.* Englewood Cliffs, NJ: Prentice-Hall.

Bandura, A. (1982). The psychology of chance encounters and life paths. *American Psychologist, 37*(7), 747-753.

Bandura, A. (Ed). (1971). *Psychological modeling: Conflicting theories.* New York: Atherton.

Barker, R. G., & Wright, H. F. (1951). *One boy's day: A specimen record of behavior.* New York: Harper.

Bettelheim, B. (1950). *Love is not enough.* New York: The Free Press.

Bettelheim, B. (1979). *Uses of enchantment.* New York: Knopf.

Bower, E. (1960). *The early identification of children with educational handicaps.* Springfield, IL: Charles C. Thomas.

Brendtro, L., Brokenleg, M., & Van Bockern, S. (2002). *Reclaiming children and youth: Our hope for the future.* Bloomington, IN: Solution Tree.

Brendtro, L., du Toit, L., Bath, H., & Van Bockern, S. (2006). Developmental Audits with challenging youth. *Reclaiming Children and Youth, 15*(4), 138-146.

Brendtro, L., & du Toit, L. (2005). *Response Ability Pathways.* Cape Town: Pretext.

Brendtro, L., & Larson, S. (2006*). The resilience revolution.* Bloomington, IN: Solution Tree.

Brendtro, L., & Long, N. (2005). Psychoeducation in the life space. *Reclaiming Children and Youth, 14*(3), 157-159.

Brendtro, L., Mitchell, M., & McCall, H. (In press). *Deep brain learning.* Albion, MI: Starr Commonwealth and Circle of Courage Institute.

Brendtro, L., & Shahbazian, M. (2004). *Troubled children and youth: Turning problems into opportunities.* Champaign, IL: Research Press.

Bronfenbrenner, U. (Ed.). (2005). *Making human beings human: Bioecological perspectives on human development.* Thousand Oaks, CA: Sage Publications.

Bronfenbrenner, U. (1979). *The ecology of human development.* Cambridge, MA: Harvard University Press.

Bullock, L., & Gable, R. (Eds.). (1999). *What works for children and youth with E/BD: Linking yesterday and today with tomorrow.* Reston, VA: Council for Exceptional Children.

Bullock, L., & Menendez, A. (1999). *Historical chronology of the Council for Children with Behavioral Disorders 1964-1999.* Reston, VA: Council for Exceptional Children.

Cohen, A. K. (1955). *Delinquent boys: The culture of the gang.* Glencoe, IL: The Free Press.

Cruickshank, W. (1972). Foreword. In J. Kauffman & C. Lewis (Eds.), *Teaching children with behavior disorders: Personal Perspectives* (pp. iii-xi). Columbus, OH: Charles E. Merrill.

Dawson, C. (2003). A study of the effectiveness of Life Space Crisis Intervention for students identified with emotional disturbances. *Reclaiming Children and Youth, 11*(4), 223-230.

Dowling, A. M. (2006). *A pictorial history of the University of Michigan Fresh Air Camp 1921-2005.* Ann Arbor: University of Michigan Press.

Forthun, L., & McCombie, J. (2007). A preliminary outcome study of Response Ability Pathways training. *Reclaiming Children and Youth, 16*(2), 27-34.

Fraiberg, S. (1968). *The magic years.* New York: Scribner.

Freud, A. (1966-1980).*The writings of Anna Freud: 8 Volumes.* New York: IUP.

Friedan, B. (1964). *The feminine mystique.* New York: Dell.

Friend, M., & Cook, L. (1997). Student-centered teams in schools: Still in search of an identity. *Journal of Educational and Psychological Consultation, 8*(1), 3-20.

Gold, M., & Osgood, D. W. (1992). *Personality and peer influence in juvenile corrections.* Westport, CT: Greenwood.

Grosenick, J. K., George, M. P., & George, N. L. (1987, May). A profile of school programs for the behaviorally disordered: Twenty years after Morse, Cutler and Fink. *Behavioral Disorders, 12*(2), 159-167.

Gump, P. V. (1955). Activity setting and social interaction. *American Journal of Orthopsychiatry, 25,* 755-60.

Gump, P. V., & Barker, R. G. (1964). *Big school, small school: High school size and student behavior.* Stanford, CA: Stanford University Press.

Gump, P. V., Schoggen, P., & Redl, F. (1957). The camp and its immediate effects. *Journal of Social Issues, 13*(1)40-46.

Heilbut, A. (1983). *Exiled in paradise: German refugee artists and intellectuals in America from 1930s to the present.* New York: Viking Press.

Hewitt, L. E., & Jenkins, R. L. (1946). *Fundamental patterns of maladjustment: The dynamics of their origin.* Ann Arbor, MI: Michigan Child Guidance Institute.

Hobbs, N. (1982). *The troubled and troubling child.* San Francisco: Jossey-Bass.

Hoffman, M. (2000). *Empathy and moral development: Implications for caring and justice.* Cambridge, UK: Cambridge University Press.

James, A. B. (2008). Roots: The life space pioneers. *Reclaiming Children and Youth, 17*(2), (4-10).

Jenkins, R. (1958). Treatment considerations. In I. A. Weeks, *Youthful offenders at Highfields* (pp. 149-156). Ann Arbor: University of Michigan Press.

Kauffman, J. M., & Lewis, C. D. (1974). *Teaching children with behavior disorders: Personal perspectives.* Columbus, OH: Charles E. Merrill Publishing Company.

Key, E. (1909). *The century of the child.* New York: G. P. Putnam's Sons.

Knitzer, J., Steinberg, Z., & Fleisch, B. (1990). *At the schoolhouse door: An examination of programs and policies for children with behavioral and emotional problems.* New York: Bank Street College of Education.

Koehler, N. (2006). Team planning to CLEAR up problems. *Reclaiming Children and Youth, 15*(3), 155-161.

Kopp, S. (1976). *If you meet the Buddha on the road, kill him!* New York: Bantam.

Korczak, J. (1967). *Janusz Korczak: Collected works.* Warsaw, Poland: United Nations.

Kounin, J., & Gump, P. (1961). The comparative influence of punitive and non-punitive teachers upon children's concepts of school misconduct. *Journal of Educational Psychology, 53*(1), 43-48.

Lantieri, L. (2001). *Schools with spirit: Nurturing the inner lives of children and teachers.* Boston: Beacon Press.

Laursen, E. (2008). Respectful alliances. *Reclaiming Children and Youth, 17*(1), 4-9.

Lewin, K. (1948). *Resolving social conflicts.* New York: Harper & Row.

Lippitt, R. & White, R. (1943). The "social climate" of children's groups. In R. Barker, J. Kounin, & H. Wright (Eds.), *Child behavior and development: A course of representative studies* (pp. 485-508). New York: McGraw-Hill.

Lloyd, J., & Kauffman, J. (January 28, 2008) Tribute to William C. Morse. Link to ebdblog.com/2008/01/28/william-c-morse

Long, N., Wood, M., & Fecser, F. (2002). *Life Space Crisis Intervention.* Austin, TX: PRO-ED Publishers.

Long, N. J., Morse, W. C., Fecser, F., & Newman, R. G. (2007). *Conflict in the classroom: The education of at-risk and troubled students* (6th ed.). Austin, TX: PRO-ED.

Maccoby, E. E., & Jacklin, C. N. (1974). *The psychology of sex differences.* Stanford, CA: Stanford University Press.

Mandela, N. (2003). A fabric of care. In K. Asmal, D. Chidester, & W. James (Eds.), *Nelson Mandela: From freedom to the future* (pp. 416-418). Johannesburg: Jonathan Ball Publishers.

McCluskey, K., & Mays, A. (2004). *Mentoring for talent development.* Sioux Falls, SD: Reclaiming Youth International.

McCorkle, L., Elias, A., & Bixby, F. (1958). *The Highfields story: An experimental treatment project for youthful offenders.* New York: Henry Holt.

McNeil, E. B. (1962). Forty years of childhood: The University of Michigan Fresh Air Camp 1921-1961. *Michigan Quarterly Review, 1*(2), 112-118.

Montessori, M. (1948). *The absorbent mind.* New York: Holt.

Morse, W. C. (1996). Involvement in the E/BD field. In B. Brooks & D. Sabatino (Eds.), *Personal perspectives on emotional disturbance/behavioral disorders* (pp. 251-271). Austin, TX: PRO-ED.

Morse, W.C. (1992). *Oral History Agreement.* Washington, DC: Council for Exceptional Children. (Interview conducted by Rosemary Nagel, December 17-18, 1991.)

Morse, W. C. (1989). Education and the emotionally/behaviorally disordered student: A personal perspective. In S. Braaten, F. Wood, & G. Wrobel (Eds.), *Celebrating the past: Preparing for the future* (pp. 23-34). Minneapolis, MN: Minnesota Council for Children with Behavioral Disorders and Minnesota Educators for Emotionally/Behaviorally Disturbed.

Morse, W. C. (1985). *The education and treatment of socioemotionally impaired youth.* Syracuse, NY: Syracuse University Press.

Morse, W. C. (1974). Dust jacket copy to H. Vorrath & L. Brendtro, *Positive Peer Culture.* Chicago: Aldine Publishing Company.

Morse, W. C. (1974). Personal perspectives. In J. Kauffman & C. Lewis (Eds.), *Teaching children with behavior disorders* (pp.198-217). Columbus, OH: Charles E. Merrill.

Morse. W., Cutler, R., & Fink, A. (1964). *Public school classes for the emotionally handicapped: A research analysis.* Washington, DC: Council for Exceptional Children, NEA.

Morse, W. C., & Smith, J. N. (1980). *Understanding child variance.* Washington, DC: CEC.

Morse, W. C., & Wingo, G. M. (1969). *Psychology and teaching.* New York: Scott, Foresman and Company.

Opp, G., & Unger, N. (2006). *Kinder stärken kinder.* Hamburg: Körber-Stiftung.

Osgood, D. W. (2006). Peer effects in juvenile justice. In K. Dodge, T. Dishion, & J. Lansford (Eds.), *Deviant peer influences in programs for youth (pp. 141-161).* New York: Guilford Press.

Peterson, C., & Seligman, M. (2004). *Character strengths and virtues: A handbook of classification.* New York: Oxford University Press.

Phelan, J. (2004). Some thoughts on using an ecosystem perspective. *CYC-Online,* Issue 28. www.cyc-net.org

Redl, F. (1976/1994). The oppositional child and the confronting adult: A mind to mind encounter. In E. J. Anthony & D. C. Gilpin (Eds.), *Clinical faces of childhood* (Vol. 1, pp. 41-58). Northvale, NJ: Jason Aronsen.

Redl, F. (1966). *When we deal with children.* New York: The Free Press.

Redl, F., & Wineman, D. (1957). *The aggressive child.* Glencoe, IL: The Free Press.

Redl, F., & Wineman, D. (1952). *Controls from within.* Glencoe, IL: The Free Press.

Redl, F., & Wineman, David. (1951). *Children who hate.* Glencoe, IL: The Free Press.

Rhodes, W. (1972). *Behavioral threat and community response.* New York: Behavioral Publications.

Rhodes, W. (1972). *Child variance: A study of childhood variance* (Vols. 1-5). Ann Arbor, MI: University of Michigan.

Schmuck, R., & Schmuck, P. (2001). *Group processes in the classroom, (8th edition).* Boston: McGraw Hill.

Seita, J., & Brendtro, L. (2005). *Kids who outwit adults.* Bloomington, IN: Solution Tree.

Seligman, M., & Czikszentmihalyi, M. (2000). Positive psychology: An introduction. *American Psychologist, 55*(1), 5-14.

Smith, L. (2004). A retrospective review of *The Aggressive Child:* An early and major exemplar of qualitative inquiry. *Qualitative Social Work, 3*(2), 221-231.

Tolan, P. H., & Cohler, B. (Eds.). (1993). *Handbook of clinical research and practice with adolescents.* New York: John Wiley and Sons.

Thrasher, F. (1927). *The gang.* Chicago: The University of Chicago Press.

Trieschman, A., Whittaker, J., & Brendtro, L. (1969). *The other 23 hours.* Chicago: Aldine.

Tyler, L. (1983). *Thinking creatively: A new approach to psychology and individual lives.* San Francisco: Jossey-Bass.

Villa, R., & Thousand, J. (2000). *Restructuring for caring and effective education.* Baltimore: Paul H. Brooks.

Vorrath, H., & Brendtro, L. (1974/1985). *Positive Peer Culture.* New York: Transaction Publishers.

Wasmund, W., & Tate, T. (2000). *Partners in empowerment.* Albion, MI: Starr Commonwealth.

Weeks, H. A. (1958). *Youthful offenders at Highfields: An evaluation of the effects of short-term treatment of delinquent boys.* Ann Arbor: The University of Michigan Press.

White, R., & Lippitt, R. (1960). *Autocracy and democracy: An experimental inquiry.* New York: Harper.

Williams, B. A. (1998). *Thought and action: John Dewey at the University of Michigan.* Ann Arbor, MI: The Bentley Historical Library, University of Michigan.

Wineman, D. (1960). Book reviews: Youthful Offenders at Highfields. *Social Work, XX,*120.

Wood, M., Brendtro, L., Fecser, F., & Nichols, P. (1999). *Psychoeducation: An idea whose time has come.* Reston, VA: Council for Exceptional Children.

Wozner, Y. (1982). Assessing the quality of internat life. *Human Relations, 35*(11), 1059-1072.

Young, L. (1966). *Life among the giants.* New York: McGraw-Hill.

Editorial Notations
Chapters One through Eight

[1]These memoirs are primarily drawn from an interview with William C. Morse conducted by Rosemary Nagel in Tampa, Florida, December 17 and 18, 1991. Additional interviews were conducted by Larry Brendtro and Adrienne Brant James in 2007 and 2008. This material is reproduced in accordance with conditions of the Oral History Agreement between the Council for Exceptional Children and William C. Morse dated Nov. 17, 1992. Permission was granted by William C. Morse for Reclaiming Children and Youth, Inc., to reproduce this material as part of a book on the contributions of the author in preparation for the Roots and Wings Conference, Wayne State University, September 18-20, 2008.

[2]WASP (White Anglo Saxon Protestant), commonly used in earlier times to describe an "all-white" setting or community.

[3]William Shakespeare, English playwright of many classics.

[4]Arthur Miller, Playwright, *All My Sons, The Crucible, Death of a Salesman,* University of Michigan alumnus for whom the Arthur Miller Theatre is named.

[5]Hammurabi –1795-1750 BC: The ruler who chiefly established the greatness of Babylon, the world's first metropolis. By far the most remarkable of the Hammurabi records is his code of laws, the earliest-known example of a ruler proclaiming publicly to his people an entire body of laws, arranged in orderly groups, so that all men might read and know what was required of them.

[6]Urie Bronfenbrenner – 1917-2005, father of Head Start, developed and published ecological theory in 1979 in *The Ecology of Human Development,* his classic and landmark book.

[7]Friends Service Summer, American Friends Service Committee (AFSC), Quaker organization that carries out programs devoted to service, development, social justice, peace throughout the world since 1917. www.afsc.org

[8]Betty Friedan – 1921–2006, American feminist, activist and writer, best known for starting what is commonly known as the "second wave" of feminism through her book *The Feminine Mystique* (1965).

[9]League of Women Voters of Michigan, Statewide umbrella for the civic participation and election reform advocacy organization.

[10]Bandura, 1982.

[11]National Youth Administration (NYA) is a former U.S. government agency established in 1935 within the Works Progress Administration; it was transferred in 1939 to the Federal Security Agency and was placed in 1942 under the War Manpower Commission. Created in a period of widespread unemployment as part of the New Deal program of President Franklin Delano Roosevelt, the NYA at first engaged in obtaining part-time work for unemployed youths. As unemployment decreased and war approached, emphasis was gradually shifted to training youths for war work until, early in 1942, all NYA activities not contributing to the war effort were dropped. Its activities ceased late in 1943.

[12] Anderson & Dearborn, 1952.

[13] McClusky, Howard Y., Professor, University of Michigan College of Education. Promoted and researched the concept of the community council, an integrating agency which unites community resources and organizations for the provision of adult education.

[14] Morse, 1974.

[15] Aichhorn, 1925; Freud, 1966-1980.

[16] Progressive Education Association, founded 1919, primarily by Francis Parker and John Dewey, progressive education movement disintegrated in the 1950s but has revived in several forms since.

[17] Wayne State University, public institution of higher learning located in Detroit Michigan; locus of initial practice and research projects initiated by Fritz Redl.

[18] Rabinovitch, Ralph D., psychiatrist, FAC, founder with wife Sara Dubo, consultant to Fresh Air Camp for several years; Hawthorn Center study.

[19] Fraiberg, Selma, FAC, author of *The Magic Years* and one of first staffers of Redl's group programs in Detroit.

[20] Cohen, Albert K., 1918-1993, FAC, criminologist best known for his subcultural theory of delinquent gangs. In 1993 Cohen received the Edwin H. Sutherland Award from the American Society of Criminology for his out-standing contributions to criminological theory and research, "status frustration and reaction formation" in *Delinquent Boys, The Culture of the Gang*.

[21] Cohler, Bertram, FAC, author of *Handbook of Clinical Research and Practice with Adolescents*, 1993 with Patrick H. Tolan.

[22] Wineman, David, FAC, clinical director of Fresh Air Camp; author with Fritz Redl of *Children who Hate* (1951) and *Controls from Within* (1952), which were combined in *The Aggressive Child* (1957).

[23] Bruno Bettelheim – 1903-90. Sonia Shankman Orthogenic School, University of Chicago residential institution for treatment of children and youth with severe emotional disturbances, controversial director. Author: *Love Is Not Enough, Uses of Enchantment*.

[24] Thrasher, 1927, classic study of Chicago gangs.

[25] *Peter and the Wolf*, composition by Sergei Prokofiev written in 1936 after his return to the Soviet Union, a children's story (with both music and text by Prokofiev), spoken by a narrator accompanied by orchestra.

[26] Bettelheim, 1972.

[27] Gump, Paul V. FAC research: Author of "The Camp and Its Immediate Effects" with Phil Schoggen and Fritz Redl (1957); "Activity Setting and Social Interaction" (1955). Author of classic *Big School, Small School: High School Size and Student Behavior*, with Roger G. Barker (1964).

[28] Life space interview. Through their work with troubled youth, Fritz Redl and David Wineman developed the "life space interview", an approach of related strategies for helping children work through – and learn from – their upsets and life crises. Underlying the Life Space Interview, or LSI, is the assumption that with support, even children with severe problems possess the resources to

understand and change their behavior. Redl and Wineman also believed that if troubled children are to be helped, immediate adult intervention is needed when crises occur. This is because people are more accepting of "new" ways of thinking -- and of behaving -- at times of duress. A crisis was regarded as an opportunity to be used for the betterment of the child. From www.psychoed.net See also *The Aggressive Child* (1957).

[29]Morse, 1985. The most extensive discussion of the life space interview is: Long, Fecser, & Wood, 2001.

[30]Morse, Cutler, & Fink, 1964, p. 131.

[31]One of the early programs was headed by Frances Lord at Eastern Michigan University. Kristen Juul from Western Michigan University and James Crowner from Michigan State University were both active in the foundation of the Council for Children with Behavioral Disorders. Central Michigan University, Wayne State University, and the University of Michigan also developed programs for teachers of disturbed children making Michigan the early leader in this field.

[32]They co-authored several editions of a text for this training: Morse & Wingo, 1969.

[33]Children's Psychiatric Hospital at University of Michigan.

[34]Dubo, Sara, psychiatrist, co-founder with husband, Ralph D. Rabinovitch, of Hawthorn Center.

[35]Hawthorn Center is a children's psychiatric hospital operated by the State of Michigan Department of Community Health, established in 1956. Under the founding leadership of Drs. Ralph Rabinovitch and Sara Dubo, Hawthorn Center has provided services to over 30,000 children and adolescents. The hospital, located in Northville Township, Michigan, has received national recognition for its innovative treatment programs, including its inpatient therapeutic milieu, day treatment program, and specialized services for preschoolers and for patients with deafness. In addition, Hawthorn Center has provided education and training to generations of mental health professionals, including psychiatrists, psychologists, social workers, nurses and special educators.

[36]Livonia, city adjacent to Detroit, Michigan, on the west side.

[37]CCBD, Council for Children with Behavioral Disorders, an international professional organization dedicated to improving educational practices for children with emotional and behavior disorders. www.ccbd.net

[38]Bower, 1960.

[39]Ortho – *American Journal of Orthopsychiatry.*

[40]MAEDC – Michigan Association for Emotionally Disturbed Children is the nation's longest operating parent activist organization. It was founded by Ralph Rabinovitch, Sara Dubo, Fritz Redl, and William Morse and directed for four decades by Sam Davis. It now operates as Michigan Association for Children with Behavior Disorders.

[41]Morse, Cutler, & Fink, 1964.

[42]Morse, 1989.

[43]Grosenick, George, & George, 1987.

[44]Knitzer, Steinberg, & Fleisch, 1990.

[45]DSM – Diagnostic and Statistical Manual of Mental Disorders, several editions. American handbook for mental health professionals that lists different categories of mental disorders and the criteria for diagnosing them, published by the American Psychiatric Association. www.psych.org

[46]U.S. Public Law 94-142 (1975). Education of All Handicapped Children Act now called Individuals with Disabilities Education Act (IDEA).

[47]Morse, 1985, p. 2.

[48]Rhodes, 1972.

[49]Morse & Smith, 1980.

[50]There is a workbook with exercises for people to use to understand these different ideas that Rhodes had presented in Child Variance.

[51]Nicholas Hobbs – 1915-83, founder of Re-ED, American Re-Education Association (AREA), pioneer in the field of child psychology and groups, first director of selection and research for the Peace Corps.

[52]Maccoby & Jacklin, 1974.

[53]Kopp,1976.

[54]Long, Morse, Fecser, & Newman, 2007.

[55]Young, 1966.

[56]Association of Educational Therapists (AET), national organization. www.aetonline.org

[57]Morse & Wingo, 1969, p. 300.

[58]For a discussion of this theme, see Morse, 1985.

[59]Morse, 1996, p. 251.

[60]Friend & Cook, 1997.

[61]IEP (Individual Education Plan). Planning required by law under the Individuals with Disabilities Education Act (P.L. 94-142), IEPC (IEP Committee), IEPT (IEP Team).

[62]Tyler, 1983.

[63]Barker & Wright, 1952.

[64]The "life space" as originally defined by Kurt Lewin refers to the person in a specific ecology where various social, psychological, and biological forces exert influence on behavior. Redl was a close colleague of Lewin and used this term to describe how the behavior of children is influenced by his or her immediate milieu or life space. The life space interview seeks to understand how the child views his or her world and copes with challenges.

[65]Morse, 1996.

[66]Long, Morse, Fecser, & Newman, 2007.

[67]Morse, 1996, p. 270.

[68]These recommendations are drawn from a chapter by William Morse in a book of the reflections by pioneers in special education for troubled children. See Kauffman & Lewis, 1974, pp. 198-217.

[69]Morse, 1996, p. 269.

∽

Epilogue Notations

[1]Letter to Robert Hook in 1675 or 1676, a tribute to Hook and Descartes.

[2]These include Jacob Kounin, who wrote widely on group discipline in class-rooms, and Paul Gump, who researched group activities and school size. Ron Lippitt brought Lewin's Center for Group Dynamics to Michigan and Theodore Newcomb became a leader in social psychology. Henry Maier helped develop the profession of child and youth care. Selma Fraiberg became a noted child therapist and author of *The Magic Years*. Albert Cohen wrote *Delinquent Boys: The Culture of the Gang*. Leon Festinger did research on cognitive dissonance. It would take another book just to review the hundreds of distinguished scholars and practitioners in this tradition.

[3]Interview by Larry Brendtro with Ralph Rabinovitch, Livonia, Michigan, May 13, 2008. The Michigan Association for Emotionally Disturbed Children which he and colleagues founded was headed for 40 years by Sam Davis; it now is named the Michigan Association for Children with Emotional Disorders.

[4]Inscription is in a personal copy from the library of Urie Bronfenbrenner.

[5]Training in the Re-ED model is provided by the American Re-Education Association directed by Mark Freado [www.re-ed.org]. Pressley Ridge operates internationally with headquarters in Pittsburgh, Pennsylvania. [www.pressleyridge.org]. The Positive Education Program provides day treatment and special education services for the city of Cleveland [www.pepcleve.org].

[6]Harry Vorrath chose the term Positive Peer Culture to distinguish this from Guided Group Interaction programs, some of which developed a highly confrontational style. Many reviews of the literature confuse these models, but bona fide Positive Peer Culture programs specifically reject peer confrontation in favor of peer concern and peer helping.

[7]For information on this journal, see [www.reclaiming.com].

[8]The Child and Youth Care website is operated by Brian Gannon, Thom Garfat, and Leon Fulcher [www.cyc-net.org].

[9]The psychoeducational website is operated by Dr. Charles Chrystal [www.psychoED.net]